BA

or

JERUSALEM

YOUR CHOICE

To Nick & Joy
Live by Revelation, not rules.

John has also written:

THE UNLEASHED CHURCH

BABYLON

or

JERUSALEM

YOUR CHOICE

John J Sweetman

Grafted

All Bible verses are from the New Living Translation (NLT) unless indicated differently.

Published in Great Britain by **Grafted**

www.graftedbydesign.co.uk

ISBN: 978-1-908569-00-4

CONTENTS

PART TWO

JERUSALEM

1.0 Introduction

Acknowledgements & Disclaimers

A book is a personal contribution but it is the result of the interaction of the lives of many people. This book is no different. The content, ideas, and vision are solely the fruit of the Holy Spirit. He has sowed seeds using many people and situations over many years. My appreciation and thanks go to those that I know and remember as well as those I have forgotten.

Special thanks to Philip for his hard work and love in helping with the words, grammar, and presentation.

I also thank Fiona and the friends who have read the manuscript. I received any helpful comments gratefully.

Any inaccuracies are my responsibility.

Preface

In the decade ending the 20th century and at the commencement of the next, a number of people gave prophecies relating to my life. These prophecies came from different people and often "out of the blue" when I was not expecting them. The person giving the prophecy usually did not know me and had not met me previously. I did not know anything was about to happen, until the person pointed at me and said they had something to say. This was common practice in a season when God restored the prophetic gift to His people.

The words were about my role in a new season – the next move of God. When I received those words, I put them in the perspective in which I lived at the time - into a known frame of reference. Since then, however, I have been able to understand much better what God was saying, as much that God spoke to me about in those prophetic words has started to come to pass. I am beginning to understand what the next move of God really means. Part of that move is an urgent call to the people of God to come out of the place that God calls

Babylon, for the tragedy is that many Christians do not know that Babylon is binding them. I did not realise that myself for much of my Christian life; when I received the prophetic words I have touched upon, I was living in Babylon. I knew no different. But no Christian man or woman would live in Babylon if they knew that was the reality of their life - and the purpose of this book is to reveal what Babylon is.

It can be read either on its own or as companion to an earlier book I wrote 'The Unleashed Church'."

Introduction

When I first heard the phrase, "Change is here to stay" I wondered what it meant. Change infers alteration, "to stay" the opposite. The truth is, we live in a changing world, and change is a constant within our environment.

Words are a constant reminder that life is full of change. Even the meanings of the words are constantly changing. The word 'gay' means something different to its meaning 100 years ago. Then, gay described a person who was 'lively' or 'merry.' Now it means someone who is lesbian or homosexual. Again, in Shakespeare's day when a character is said to be arriving 'presently' that character is arriving immediately. Nowadays we use 'presently' to indicate that something will happen soon.

The word "Church" did not exist 2000 years ago. There were other words used to give definition to the people of God such as 'ecclesia'- meaning the called out ones. The writers of the New Testament explained their experience in words that did not conjure up the concepts we now imagine when we read those same words in the English translations of the bible. Today, the word "Church" evokes buildings, structures, laws, and definitions all far removed from the understanding of the early followers of Jesus.

The meaning of the word "Babylon" has undergone similar change. To early inhabitants of the world's cities, Babylon was a centre of commerce. It became a powerful military force, conquering much of the world. In John's day, he and the other disciples understood differently and this book explores what he understood. Since then, Christians have put an ever-different interpretation on "Babylon", often using the name as a weapon against the followers of an alternative group. Speak to a Muslim, and he will give his own perspective.

In his vision, written in the book of Revelation, John states that God's people must come out of Babylon or He will destroy them with her. It is vital, therefore, that we understand what the word means, or we may find destruction at the end of our journey.

The purpose of this book is to explore the meaning of "Babylon", to understand its character, and to consider God's alternative city, Jerusalem, that He asks us to find.

Part One

Babylon

The Beginning

There are many word pictures in the bible. The writers used them to describe and bring clarity to the issues they dealt with and often used opposing pictures to polarise their thoughts and ideas. For example, in Galatians 4 we read that two women, Sarah and Hagar, represent the Old and New Covenants. They are important figures in Scripture, but it is not immediately apparent that the account of their lives means so much. However, we have to see this in order to understand the purpose of their stories being in Scripture. The Holy Spirit is not just giving their history, but giving a purpose in their history. If the lives of these two women can mean something so expansive, should we not wonder if other accounts in Scripture mean much more than may be obvious at first?

A picture of the kingdom of God is Jerusalem while a picture of the kingdom of Satan is Babylon. For us to understand what these pictures mean we have to search into their usage in the bible.

The bible is full of accounts of the history of kingdoms; all but one belongs to the secular world. The exception is the Kingdom belonging to God Himself. The Book of Revelation shows the destiny of all those secular kingdoms – destruction. Only the Kingdom of Heaven will survive and bring salvation.

Given this, it is imperative we know to which kingdom we belong. Revelation 18:4 states clearly that many of God's people are in Babylon and have to escape if they are not to perish with her. *"Then I heard another voice calling from heaven, "Come away from her, my people. Do not take part in her sins, or you will be punished with her."* Paul, in his letter to the people of God in Corinth, explains that many will have all that they have worked for destroyed as if it were wood, hay, or stubble. I fear that many who have built great empires in the church today will see all that they have constructed suffer a similar fate.

There has always been speculation by people who read the bible as to the identity of Babylon. Many strive to see a particular nation or organisation as the modern day fulfilment of the biblical prophecies about it. In fact, what is important to stress is that there are only two kingdoms, pictured as two cities: Jerusalem or Babylon. Anything that is not Jerusalem is Babylon. The cities each manifest the character of these two kingdoms and while there is not a particular nation or organisation that is Babylon, the characteristics of that city are evidenced in the spirit that controls its citizens. It is this character, or spirit, from which we have to escape.

The book of Genesis shows the beginnings of many of these kingdoms. Beginnings are significant because they set the course for the future development. Let me give a simple illustration. Put a plant into a pot and it will grow, in strength and in health, only as far as the dimensions of that pot allow. Similarly with a kingdom. For example, consider the beginnings of Babylon and Jerusalem. Each has grown according to its initial founding; the way in which each was planted.

1.0 Babylon -The Roots
Genesis 10:8-10 tells us that the city of Babylon was built through the efforts of one of the sons of Cush, a

man named Nimrod who was a mighty hunter. *" Cush was also the ancestor of Nimrod, who was the first heroic warrior on earth. Since he was the greatest hunter in the world, his name became proverbial. People would say, "This man is like Nimrod, the greatest hunter in the world." He built his kingdom in the land of Babylonia, with the cities of Babylon, Erech, Akkad, and Calneh. "* The bible does not tell us specifically whether he was a good man or not, just that he was a mighty warrior / hunter. However, the name Nimrod means rebel and Babylon was the first centre from which he moved. Both these facts indicate something of his character.

Babylon means the Gate of God. In Genesis 3:24, we read, *"After sending them out, the Lord God stationed mighty cherubim to the east of the Garden of Eden. And he placed a flaming sword that flashed back and forth to guard the way to the tree of life."* God's judgement was that man must not enter Eden again. Nimrod, being a rebel, opposed that judgement and built a city named "The Gate of God". In doing so, perhaps Nimrod was declaring his ability to create an environment equal to Eden itself, or that his city provided an alternative gate to the one sealed by God.

Genesis 10:10 states," *Nimrod was an empire builder*". Empire building is a characteristic of those who want to build a monument to their own image. Nimrod headed up a great confederacy of peoples against God, aiming to establish a world empire, having its centre at Babel. A dictionary defines an empire as *"a group of nations, territories, or peoples ruled by a single authority, especially an emperor or empress"*. An empire is the result of many kingdoms coming together, usually through oppression or manipulation. One individual rules an empire. The desire for empire is a corruption of the character of God. God told Adam to nurture His creation (Gen 2:15) *"The Lord God placed the man in the Garden of Eden to tend and watch over it"*. God did not give Adam freedom to rule over a kingdom. He asked him to enjoy life within His kingdom. Nimrod, however, wanted to rule over man. He built his own kingdom. Not satisfied with that, he conquered and then ruled over many kingdoms.

The heart of "empire" is in many church groups today. I read an email recently from a leader of a group of churches. His desire was to grow a large group of churches and he was encouraging people to register their individual churches on his web site. He already counted 400 churches but wanted more. The inevitable result of empire is control and manipulation.

Genesis 11 tells us *"At one time all the people of the world spoke the same language and used the same words. As the people migrated to the east, they found a plain in the land of Babylonia and settled there. They began saying to each other, "Let's make bricks, and harden them with fire." (In this region, bricks were used instead of stone, and tar was used for mortar.) Then they said, "Come, let's build a great city for ourselves with a tower that reaches into the sky. This will make us famous and keep us from being scattered all over the world." But the Lord came down to look at the city and the tower the people were building. "Look!" he said.*

"The people are united, and they all speak the same language. After this, nothing they set out to do will be impossible for them! Come, let us go down, and confuse the people with different languages. Then they won't be able to understand each other." In that way, the Lord scattered them all over the world, and they stopped building the city. That is why the city was called Babel, because that is where the Lord confused the people with different languages. In this way, he scattered them all over the world."

Nimrod's followers built the tower of Babel on the plains of Babylonia. Babel was the first visible sign that Babylon had begun. The character of Babel builders is significant.

- 11:1 They were settlers in Babylonia
- 11:2 They were plain dwellers
- 11:3 They used bricks instead of stone (man-made uniformity and control)
- 11:4 They used asphalt as mortar (man- made adhesive)
- 11:5 They built a city

- 11:6 They had a desire to reach to heaven and make a name for themselves (pride)
- 11:7 and not be scattered (trust in man's ability for security)
- 11:8 Confusion
- 11:9 Division

1.1 Settlers

Babylonians are settlers. On the face of it, this does not sound too bad, but if we dig under the surface, we find that settling is in opposition to the intentions of God.

Many people teach that there are two types in the world - pioneers and settlers. There are many sub categories for both these types but let us consider the general statement.

According to a Dictionary, a pioneer is *"One of those who first enter or settle in a region, thus opening it for occupation and development by others"*.

Pioneers are those who go in front. They pave the way for others to follow. They open doors, fight for new ground, take risks. They face challenges head on. They leave the familiar and secure for the unfamiliar and unknown. Pioneers are responsible for movements, expeditions, new concepts, new ideas, inventions, experiments, new territory, and new businesses.

Settlers follow after pioneers have won the victories and make the location comfortable. They do not take risks. They avoid challenges. They stay together in order to make a place secure and risk free. Settlers construct the laws, establish the boundaries, and build the educational and financial systems.

Settlers are not necessarily "bad" people. It is simply that their character stops a forward movement. That is fine if we have arrived at the destination, but fatal if we are still on the journey. There is a difference between settling and consolidation. To consolidate is important after a time of moving into new territory; important as a time for recovery and building up resources for the next move forwards. But, when the consolidation becomes settling the forward movement stops.

History is full of the tragedy of settlers who have brought a forward movement to a standstill. Take the biblical history of Israel. God raised up Moses, as a pioneer, to take the nation out of slavery and into a new land, as outlined in the book of Exodus. He was a true pioneer. But he had a major problem – the people did not want to follow him. Initially they were glad to escape slavery and hardship in Egypt. Nonetheless, they had no stomach for pioneering. Very soon, they were looking back to Egypt with foolish desire, meeting every challenge with complaints, with fear. As a result, God destroyed a whole generation.

The next generation did break into the land but quickly settled again. Instead of obeying God and destroying the pagan nations, as He had commanded, they settled down among those nations. Soon they became indistinguishable from them. In short, as all settlers do, they became, in essence, slaves to their environment.

Again and again God raised up judges to pioneer the nation out of slavery. Yet settlers moved in almost immediately afterwards, taking the nation back into slavery. Following the Judges, God gave priests, kings, and prophets. But each time settlers prevented the nation from moving forward.

Jesus, the great Pioneer, broke the power of all captivity. Many of us, though, still settlers, prefer our natural state. We are too comfortable, or too afraid to move on. Throughout history, visionaries have started many movements, only for their followers to build walls defining boundaries they have themselves established. Boundaries behind which they can feel safe. All this reflects Babylon. Babylon loves settlers. As soon they move in, the character of Babylon takes over those that remain behind.

The writer of the book of Hebrews in chapter 12:2 calls Jesus "The great Pioneer of our faith". Many versions of the bible translate the word for "pioneer" as "author". An author is by definition creative and the emphasis in the word is in the creative nature of Jesus - His ability to begin new things. Nowhere do we read of Him given the title "The great Settler". Now, some may argue that we are called to "be at rest" in Jesus or that we are "in Christ" and this infers settling. In response, I suggest our position "In Christ" is more like that of the warriors inside the Trojan horse. They were "in the horse" but it is highly unlikely they were spending time considering the definition of the horse. They were there, and they knew they were there, for one purpose only; to take new ground as soon as the horse was opened. The parallel with us is clear. We are to be ready to take new ground at all times. Our Pioneer, Jesus, is moving forwards and we are in Him. As He moves into new territory, we go with Him ready for the battle.

God calls us to be pioneers - to press on to fulfil our calling. Until Jesus returns we cannot, we must not, settle. Both personally and corporately, we will die if we settle. Settlers crave security in knowing what they can and cannot do. To achieve this they make rules. establish boundaries. In doing so, sadly, they create new divisions in the Body of Christ.

It cannot be emphasised enough that the kingdom of God is not static. It continues to move forward. And it will continue to move forward until Jesus returns. Our security therefore should come from knowing our place in Christ, not from the rules of an organisation to which we belong.

Bearing in mind that Babylon is full of settlers each one of us needs to ask: "Am I a settler or a pioneer?"

1.2 Plain dwellers

Babylonians settle in the plains. Mountains are for people who live in Jerusalem.

The plains tend to be surrounded by mountains, or higher ground. Mountains are not good for easy habitation for large groups; it takes time to climb the mountain and the climb is difficult. Plains are wide, open, spaces with plenty of flat land to build cities.

The biblical picture of the person seeking God is of a person climbing a mountain. It seems that God designed us for living in the mountains. Jesus spent much time in the mountains where He talked to His Father and listened about forthcoming events. The mountain is where we can spend time in solitude with Father. It takes determination, time, and effort to climb mountains.

The biblical picture of the person living in defiance to or away from God is of a plain dweller. The plain is a place that is easy to reach. If you are on the mountain, you can let gravity take you down to the plain. The plain is for people who do not want to commune with God. It is a place of ease and comfort. It speaks of laziness and self-centredness.

There are many examples in the bible of the plains being a place where we are away from God. Lot, as he parted from Abraham, chose to live in the plains. He quickly fell in with ungodly people and had to be rescued by Abraham from total destruction as a result.

In Numbers 21 onwards, we read that Moses led the Israelites to the plains of Moab before entering the Promised Land. God led him to the plains as a place from which to move. When camped in the plain, Moses went up the mountain to talk to God and view the land. The people had to leave the plains in order to move into God's Promised Land. The plains were not a place to stay.

In Judges 1:19 we read that the Israelites lived in the mountains but their enemy lived in the plains. Spiritually speaking, plain dwellers are always the enemy of God's people. But God also governs the plains, as is made clear in 1 Kings 20:23. The king of Aram's advisors tell him that the God of David is a God of the hills. He should therefore fight the Israelites on the plains. He does so, and his army is wiped out. Again, in 2 Kings 25:5, we read of the Babylonian army capturing King Zedekiah of Israel on the plains of Jericho. The king had fallen low and turned his back on God. It was fitting therefore that he should meet his fate on the plains.

The Babylonians overcame Israel and took the land into captivity. Israel had stopped communing with God. In response, He sent them out of the mountain land; they no longer represented Him.

We can only have a relationship with God on a personal basis. We can share this relationship with others, but if we have no relationship with Him, we have nothing to share with others. Our relationship with God is primarily developed individually, rather than in a group. It is true that being part of a group is vital for fellowship; God talks to us through that fellowship. But we are not part of a large production line that produces the finished article one after the other. Instead, the Holy Spirit individually creates and moulds us through our relationship with Him. It is our time alone with Him on the mountain that changes and releases us into God's purposes to fulfil our destiny. Plain dwellers do not participate in this life. Sadly, many people who attend church services are plain dwellers. They have no connection to Jesus; have no relationship with Him. They attend services but are not part of Him.

Are we living on the plain without God or on the mountain with Him?

1.3 Builders using Brick

Strangely, God uses the picture of people who build with bricks to describe people who are not walking with Him. Whenever God builds, He uses stone and instructs us to use stone also. He seems to make a distinction between builders who use brick and those who use stone. In 1

Peter 2:5, He describes His people as stones in His temple. Why does He make this distinction?

He does so because there is a significant difference between the two. Brick comes from fire made by man. Brick, baked in a kiln, easily erodes and becomes brittle. God forges stone from the heat and pressure of His creation. (I accept that man does make some 'stone' used to clad the outside of buildings. But that material is not true stone.) True stone is evidence of God's handiwork. True stone is durable.

Stone talks of the work of God; brick of man's self-effort.

When building an altar, the people of God used stone. God expressly told them not to use dressed stones for an altar; they should not use any tool on it. See Ex 20:25 *"If you use stones to build my altar, use only natural, uncut stones. Do not shape the stones with a tool, for that would make the altar unfit for holy use."* God did not allow human effort in putting shape to the stones for the altar. That is God's work. He specifically forbade the use of bricks. When we worship God, He enjoys and welcomes people who come because of His work in their lives. He does not accept us with our self-righteousness but only in His Righteousness.

When building the Temple, God instructed Solomon to shape the stone outside Jerusalem before bringing it to the city, so that there would be no noise in the city. The Temple has a different use to that of the altar. Each speaks to us of different aspects of the kingdom of God. The altar speaks of worship. The Temple speaks of the people of God. God uses our relationships to change us. In doing so, He changes the shape of the stones of the "Temple".

Bricks, man-made, are uniform in shape and size. Real stone, true stone, is full of variety. Everything that God does speaks of variety - in people, flowers, trees, mountains. God rarely copies or repeats the same thing. But there is no variety in the shape and size of mass-produced bricks. They are designed to be the same in shape, size and weight so that they can be laid quickly, conveniently, uniformly.

That is why Babylon produces and uses bricks. Man closely controls the production of bricks because uniformity is vital for their use in building quickly. Much of what takes place in the organised church reflects that. People are put onto a production line of alpha groups, beta groups, cell groups, leadership training courses, counselling training, eldership training, Sunday sermons, church vision, and programmes. In doing this, whether consciously or not, leaders are likely to create people who follow their doctrines and methods; people who are the same as them – bricks. There is little freedom for the Holy Spirit to craft His stones into what He wants. Instead, the organised church forms bricks.

God is our Father and He desires for us to walk with Him. Hebrews 12:5-13 tells us that He is the one who trains us and treats us as His sons. *"And have you forgotten the encouraging words God spoke to you as his children? He said, "My child, don't make light of the Lord's discipline, and don't give up when he corrects you. For the Lord disciplines those he loves, and he punishes each one he accepts as his child." As you endure this divine discipline, remember that God is treating you as his own children. Who ever heard of a child who is never disciplined by its father? If God doesn't discipline you as he does all of his children, it means that you are illegitimate and are not really his children at all. Since we respected our earthly fathers who disciplined us, shouldn't we submit even more to the discipline of the Father of our spirits, and live forever? For our earthly fathers disciplined us for a few years, doing the best they knew how. But God's discipline is always good for us, so that we might share in his holiness. No discipline is enjoyable while it is happening—it's painful! But afterward there will be a peaceful harvest of right living for those who are trained in this way. So take a new grip with your tired hands and strengthen your weak knees. Mark out a straight path for your feet so that those who are weak and lame will not fall but become strong."*

Our purpose is not to be bricks used by man for his own purposes. Our purpose is to allow the hands of God to form us, to fit into His Temple.

Let me illustrate this. For many years, the church has used evangelistic meetings to preach the gospel. The format for the meeting may vary but usually, after a short time of sharing the way in which all listening can change their lives for good - by receiving the Holy Spirit and walking with God - the speaker will ask the group for their response. The listeners may respond by standing and raising their hands to signify they want to be "Christians". They may recite a prayer repeating the words of the speaker. At this, the "brick people" present are excited: they have new "Christians" they can report on in triumph to their church. Yet, in reality, God had not yet hewn any stone from the ground. No one has been baptized yet. It is true that some may receive the Holy Spirit and the experience is life changing but this is the exception rather than the rule. Perhaps some had their appetite sharpened for more. Perhaps someone had taken a step towards God. But, how much was stone cutting?

Man makes bricks using control techniques - of quality and quantity. Babylon loves control and achieves that by making rules. Much of what goes on in church groups is control by rules, although often those in the groups do not realise this. People do things from the best of motives. Yet, sadly, the effect is often to control the actions and beliefs of others. An example of this is the use of "church vision". This may sound sensible, perhaps even desirable, but a group that has a "church vision" has fallen into the trap of creating division and control of its members. Many, if not most, such groups will say, "If you do not agree with the vision, you should not be part of this group." In doing so, they control anyone who wants to be part of the group even if they do not agree with the vision. The reality is that there should not be a church vision. The use of such a tool, such as 'vision', immediately creates a barrier and division in the Body of Christ. Vision is an individual calling. It will be different for each one of us. We have an individual destiny as we respond to God. Certainly, this may be fulfilled by walking with others; but as soon as we limit ourselves to a particular group, we have become elitist, set apart from others.

Tithing is another control tool. I have met many people hurt by it. In many church groups, tithing is a requirement for members to be part of the group. Members pay the tithe to the leader and he or she often keeps it. The leader does not always tithe and is often the wealthiest person in the group. I have even known 'churches' where those who cannot afford to tithe have their names listed on a notice of shame for all to see. In some churches if a member has a heavy cost, such as a wedding or funeral, to bear, the church members assist them, if they have paid their tithes regularly. If they have not they get no assistance until they have made up their back payments. Many will argue that tithing is a biblical principle still valid today. It is certainly a principle in the bible. But whether it is valid today is very doubtful. At best, the only argument for it is that it applies solely to Messianic Jews who are nonetheless Jews, bound by the Torah, although believing in Yeshua as the Messiah.

It certainly does not apply to Christians from a Gentile background. Nonetheless, a Christian is encouraged to give generously. It was a common response in the first body of Christians to give away 100% of the proceeds from the sale of fields and other income. But, they did not do this out of an obligation to tithe. They did it out of generosity of spirit, wholeheartedly, free from the law of the tithe. For those who wish to investigate this point more I have attached an appendix covering the reasons why tithing is no longer necessary today.

Doctrine is another control tool – one of the many tools used to keep members within boundaries set by the leaders. Leaders frequently ask those who do not accept the doctrine of their particular church group to leave. Leaders have many control tools to use to keep their group within the boundaries they set. Such leaders, such controls, are Babylonian in character.

To repeat: bricks speak of uniformity and conformity. Stones speak of variety. The biblical expectation when the people of God meet together is of variety. In 1 Cor 14:26 we read, *"Well, my brothers and sisters, let's summarize. When you meet together, one will sing, another will teach, another will tell some special revelation God has given, one will speak in tongues, and another will interpret what is said. But everything that is done must strengthen all of you."* Everyone has something of the Holy Spirit to contribute which is different on each occasion. With Babylon, this does not happen. There is conformity and uniformity. A typical service is a collection of songs, previously selected by the leaders, prayers, often according to a given theme, and a sermon or talk to round it all up. If anyone wishes to add something not already 'programmed' a leader has to check it first.

I cannot emphasize enough that none of this procedure is found in the Bible; it is a function of the Babylonian character.

As for the 'Jerusalem' character, I will touch on that later. Meantime, as a response to the above, perhaps it is time to consider how much variety and uniqueness we have in our lives. Time to consider whether what we do is the result of the prompting of the Holy Spirit in us.

1.4 Users of mortar.

Bricks have to be cemented into position. Stones do not. Stones are shaped so that they can be laid one upon another or side by side without the need for any 'cement' as anyone who has seen dry-stones walls being built can confirm. Indeed, Stonemasons cut the stones of lighthouses so precisely that each stone fitted exactly with those either side, and above and below, often without the need for cement – imperative if the lighthouse was to resist the full force of the sea in a Force 10 gale.

In contrast, bricks are easily displaced if they are not held together by some kind of mortar or cement between them. This is a characteristic of Babylon; the group needs 'cement' of some kind to hold together, and when people are displaced, no concern is shown. Indeed, in some 'churches' when people leave, church members respond with pride. They feel they are the 'righteous' ones, now free of troublemakers. They are encouraged by their departure.

Stones are not easily moved however. They fit tightly together; so tightly that as in the lighthouse illustration above, they can resist the full force of the elements hurled against them.

And that is how we are meant to be – a Temple, not a pile of bricks.

In Jerusalem, stones are individually shaped to fit snugly with each other, without cement. In Babylon, bricks need mortar to keep them from moving; the mortar necessary because the brick is uniform with no individual character. Indeed, the 'mortar' can be likened to the unhealthy means used by certain groups to keep their members together. Means such as the personality of the leader, the doctrine of the group, or manipulation. Sometimes, a group exists because it has grown around a personality, or a doctrine. Sometimes it grows around a group of friends who feel they have something in common. But, however such groups grow often there is no spiritual bond.

It is easy to displace a brick. Perhaps through an argument over a minor issue, a personality clash, the dislike of the worship songs, or a dispute over the vision or doctrine. There are many reasons for displacing a brick.

Where a group thinks that numbers are important, they will use some kind of adhesive to keep people together. Sometimes, there will be a dumbing down of anything that might challenge conscience, to create a non-threatening environment where little of value is taught. Manipulation is another form of cement. It may be a threat that awful things will happen if a member steps out of line such as, "If you do not tithe to this group, you will have severe financial problems," or "If you leave, you will have no covering and be open to every attack Satan sends".

In contrast, the Holy Spirit holds people together. He starts to draw people to Jesus. There is no need of any kind of 'cement'. In the Holy Spirit, each one of us fits as closely, one with the other, as do the stones of a lighthouse.

God calls us to be stones in a Temple, durable, committed to relationship - not to an organisation. It is true that, as pioneers, we will constantly be moving forwards, and this might create a changing set of relationships. But they change, not through division, but through the ongoing call of God. Sometimes moving on with God means we do lose touch with people. Nonetheless, a relationship formed by the power of the Holy Spirit overcomes this difficulty and continues when those concerned next meet.

We should not be afraid of moving forward, even when it does disturb our comfort and the friendships we have. Responding to the Holy Spirit will take us into new relationships and challenges. In Babylon, relationships are broken through division. They are difficult to restore because the 'cement' between those concerned has failed. But when we are joined in relationship through the Holy Spirit nothing can get between us.

1.5 City builders

The Babylonians built a city, and historically cities had to have walls, to contain those within and repel those without. Historically the "church", however that term is defined, erected walls of procedure, content, hierarchy about it – to contain those within and exclude those without. It developed an administration to control those within its boundaries, rules, and codes of practice, a unique character with its own dialect. How many "cities" are there in the landscape of the church? Every new doctrine or revelation throughout history has caused its adherents to build a new "city". Inevitably, the walls keep the inhabitants from living elsewhere and very quickly, a new stronghold appears.

Each new "church" movement has built walls around its revelation or doctrine. Each movement has individual codes of practice. As in a walled city, there is an administration with titles and positions, giving recognition and authority to those charged with ensuring the "inhabitants" obey the rules, doctrine, and codes. Those who do not fit the unique culture of the city do not survive. They leave because either they feel like outcasts or the "city police" will ask them to go as they cause too much trouble.

The tragedy in all this is that the "church" today displays this Babylonian characteristic without realising the shame and dishonour it brings to the name of Jesus. Every "city" declares a division that breaks the unity that is the desire in the heart of Jesus.

1.6 Monument makers

The stated purpose of the Babylonians was to build a monument to themselves, to declare their greatness. It was rooted in pride. We usually associate pride with a self-centred attitude accompanied by self-effort and self-glorification. But the definition of pride is something or someone that is raised above another. A badly cut fingernail that does not have a smooth edge is said to be proud. If there are two pieces of adjoining wood and one is raised above the other, it is said to be proud. Neither of these examples includes an attitude - they are of inanimate objects - but they emphasise the rising of one above another.

We criticise pride because it is associated with the attitude of self-centredness; God rejects proud people because they are raised up, with or without an attitude. James 4:6 states that God resists the proud but exalts the humble. This is much like Isaiah who prophesied that the mountains would be laid low and the valleys raised up in preparation for the coming of the Lord. For us the implication is clear: we too are to become a level place for the Lord to inhabit. God will bring the proud down and raise the humble to the same level.

There have been, and still are, many leaders within the Church who serve with humility. Leaders who are not arrogant or self-centred. I do not seek to belittle such men and women of God; I am simply making the point that anyone who is raised above another is, by definition, 'proud'.

In Ezekiel 34 vs 1-34, a passage relating to the return of Israel to their land, we read a long prophesy against the shepherds of Israel alive at the time who were mistreating the sheep. *"Then this message came to me from the Lord: "Son of man, prophesy against the shepherds, the leaders of Israel. Give them this message from the Sovereign Lord: What sorrow awaits you shepherds who feed yourselves instead of your flocks. Shouldn't shepherds feed their sheep? You drink the milk, wear the wool, and butcher the best animals, but you let your flocks starve. You have not taken care of the weak. You have not tended the sick or bound up the injured. You have not gone looking for those who have wandered away and are lost. Instead, you have ruled them with harshness and cruelty. So my sheep have been scattered without a shepherd, and they are easy prey for any wild animal. They have wandered through all the mountains and all the hills, across the face of the earth, yet no one has gone to search for them.*

"Therefore, you shepherds, hear the word of the Lord: As surely as I live, says the Sovereign Lord, you abandoned my flock and left them to be attacked by every wild animal. And though you were my shepherds, you didn't search for my sheep when they were lost. You took care of yourselves and left the sheep to starve. Therefore, you shepherds, hear the word of the Lord. This is what the Sovereign Lord says: I now consider these shepherds my enemies, and I will hold

them responsible for what has happened to my flock. I will take away their right to feed the flock, and I will stop them from feeding themselves. I will rescue my flock from their mouths; the sheep will no longer be their prey.

"For this is what the Sovereign Lord says: I myself will search and find my sheep. I will be like a shepherd looking for his scattered flock. I will find my sheep and rescue them from all the places where they were scattered on that dark and cloudy day. I will bring them back home to their own land of Israel from among the peoples and nations. I will feed them on the mountains of Israel and by the rivers and in all the places where people live. Yes, I will give them good pastureland on the high hills of Israel. There they will lie down in pleasant places and feed in the lush pastures of the hills. I myself will tend my sheep and give them a place to lie down in peace, says the Sovereign Lord. I will search for my lost ones who strayed away, and I will bring them safely home again. I will bandage the injured and strengthen

the weak. But I will destroy those who are fat and powerful. I will feed them, yes,—feed them justice!

"And as for you, my flock, this is what the Sovereign Lord says to his people: I will judge between one animal of the flock and another, separating the sheep from the goats. Isn't it enough for you to keep the best of the pastures for yourselves? Must you also trample down the rest? Isn't it enough for you to drink clear water for yourselves? Must you also muddy the rest with your feet? Why must my flock eat what you have trampled down and drink water you have fouled?

"Therefore, this is what the Sovereign Lord says: I will surely judge between the fat sheep and the scrawny sheep. For you fat sheep pushed and butted and crowded my sick and hungry flock until you scattered them to distant lands. So I will rescue my flock, and they will no longer be abused. I will judge between one animal of the flock and another. And I will set over them one shepherd, my servant David. He will feed them and be a shepherd to them. And I, the Lord, will be their God, and my *servant David will be a prince among my people. I, the Lord, have spoken!"*

The Shepherds were feeding themselves at the cost of the sheep and God strongly rebuked them to the extent that He would destroy them. The term "sheep" was referring to people. But what was the sin of the shepherds? It would seem they acted much the same as some pastors and leaders of today's church. Verse 2 informs us that the shepherds were to feed the sheep. Instead - v3 & 4 - they drank the milk, wore the wool, and butchered the best animals whilst letting the flock starve. They did not take care of the weak. They did not tend the sick; they did not mend the bones. They left the lost to wander and no one looked for them. They ruled the sheep with force and cruelty, the absolute opposite of what God charged them to do. In v11 onwards, God clearly states that He will be the good shepherd. He will take over the shepherding care.

In John 10 Jesus re-emphasises this by declaring that He is the Good Shepherd, fulfilling this prophesy of Ezekiel. He still is the Good Shepherd. He has not relinquished or delegated the role to anyone else. Today, He shepherds through the Holy Spirit within His people, not by making an individual proud by raising him or her up. His people – those who are truly His - have the spirit to care for each other if they respond to Him.

But, how are the sins of the pastors today the same as those shepherds in Ezekiel's day? Because pastors today often still rob the sheep instead of feeding them. They may believe that they fulfil their responsibility to feed by preaching from the bible. Yet what they preach is often erroneous, as is the belief that God calls one person to teach the rest. 1 John 2:27 makes it quite clear that we do not need anyone to teach us what is true because we *".... have received the Holy Spirit, and he lives within you, so you don't need anyone to teach you what is true. For the Spirit teaches you everything you need to know, and what he teaches is true — it is not a lie. So just as he has taught you, remain in fellowship with Christ."*

The Holy Spirit is our Teacher. He lives in each of us. He teaches us directly. Having said this I must emphasise that there have been, and are still, men and women truly inspired by God, moved by the Holy Spirit, who brought, who still bring, the word of God powerfully to us.

If a person wishes to take on the role of a Pastor, he/she is required to feed the sheep. Pastors fulfil this, according to Ezekiel 34, in finding physical food not just spiritual. It would include looking after the sheep by finding employment and finance as well as food. Instead, there are so-called Pastors who live off the sheep. They rob the sheep. In Africa, for example, it is common practice for a leader of a church to insist that the church members provide them with chickens every Sunday for their personal food during the following week, even though their flock may be starving. The church members are required to tithe; money that the leader will keep to pay for their car or other luxury, even though their sheep are too poor to eat properly. The Pastor/leader claims to live by faith, and in a sense they are: but not their faith. It is the faith of the sheep.

Do pastors today heal the sick and mend their bones or send them to hospital? Do pastors today go looking for those who have wandered away? Or do they close the door on them, glad they do not have to be bothered with them anymore? Do pastors today rule with a rod of iron, making so many rules and creating doctrinal laws that people live in condemnation?

Ezekiel says that the sheep in his time were scattered. Ezek 34:5. All too often it is the same today, the scattering the result of pastors ruling badly with many sheep lost, wandering in the hills. The Babylonian character of those pastors has replaced that of Jesus.

The Babylonians built a monument to themselves. There are many such monuments in the church today. People want the biggest church in the town, or area, or even the world as a monument to what they are doing. To prove what they believe is right. Jesus, on the other hand, just wants people for Himself.

I had a conversation with a man wanting to build a large orphanage. I suggested it would be better to find many parents who were able to take the children into their families. This would enable the children to grow in an environment replicating a normal family instead of a large organisation. Much money would be saved by not building big premises; money that could be invested in the parents, to provide education, as well as helping to develop local services for the benefit of many more people. The person I was speaking to replied that he wanted to build something that would be a testimony to him. Sadly, this attitude is common.

We have a God-given desire to make a difference to the situations in which we are involved. But this is very different to the desire to leave a legacy. God should be central, as everything was created by Him and for Him. At Babel man wanted to make a name for himself, whereas God promised Abraham that He would make him a blessing, and his name is still remembered.

To repeat, something that is raised above another is, by definition, proud, attitude present or not. Leaders tend to be raised up. They do not have to be. If his or her leadership comprises someone going before, literally being in front, there is no need for the leader to be raised up. Yet our culture has a tendency to do this. Perhaps it is the search for security in position, or for satisfaction in approbation. Perhaps people are raised up against their wishes. Whatever the reason, we find pastors, apostles, prophets, teachers, evangelists, deacons, bishops et al all raised to a higher level. They become a class apart. Yet, in reality, there is only one reason for being different – and that is whether the Holy Spirit lives in us or not. If He is with us, we are different from others. It is a difference, which others should see and cause wonder.

So then, which is more important - the message or the messenger? It is - it must be - the message. Consider, if I give a message to a small child for his mother the child is not important, other than in obediently delivering the message. The person sending the message may be important, but not the messenger. Since we are all simply messengers, why raise ourselves up as if we were important? It is the message, the Word person we carry, the person who sent us, who is important.

Few people have experience of situations without leaders: the Babylonian system suffocates us wherever we turn in the secular and spiritual arenas. Although it has become the normal way for thousands of years, it is not God's way. We shall see God's way when we consider Jerusalem.

1.7 No scattering.

There is a Godly injunction to us to scatter. It started with Adam who had a mandate to occupy the whole world. It continued when Jesus told His first disciples to go into the whole world. (Gen 1:28; Acts 1:8). When we obey God, He sends us out. This is different from the scattering that occurs when we do not have the Shepherd to care for us.

Babylon resists the godly requirement to scatter. Babylon has a character that seeks to control people; to keep them within strict boundaries.

Why does God call us to scatter?

There could be many reasons. One is that by scattering we sow seed into new ground, a parallel here being the parable of the Sower. He sowed seed wherever he went, into good and poor soil alike. Some seed bore fruit that lasted. Some withered quickly. But he still sowed. The fact is that seeds will reproduce if sown into soil. They do not reproduce if kept out of soil.

The Babylonian character resists scattering and many church groups demonstrate this character. Often the culture and vision of a large church is to keep people within the membership of the same group. There is a strong desire that those people stay together, because of the assumption that the group is right in all things - doctrine and practice. The issue of pride apart, this is also wrong; it is seeking to control people. Such churches teach people to submit to the leader whether that leader is right or wrong. They teach that submission is more important than personally hearing God. In teaching this, leaders are controlling the people who submit to them.

A common teaching is that one should submit to another's vision in order eventually to gain a vision for oneself. Again, this teaching enables leaders to control people. An individual is not allowed to have his or her own vision unless the leaders are happy with it. Such teaching, such control of the flock, also stops people from scattering.

It is common for people with a Babylonian emphasis to accuse a Christian of backsliding if he or she is not in a submissive relationship to a leader. This is both unhelpful and contrary to the truth, which we will consider further when we look at Jerusalem.

Meantime, there are many ways in which leaders control people, often without intention. Terms like "Discipleship", "Mentoring", "Coaching" and "House Church" sound very good but are not always helpful. They can produce stereotypes of the leader and a way to control the behaviour of people. Having said that, it is true that Jesus instructed His first disciples to go into all the world and make disciples of the nations (Matthew 28:17). But the discipleship that Jesus intended was different to that of the churches. Jesus expects us to be His disciples - not disciples of people.

The Babylonian church does allow some people to scatter - eventually. A Mother Church will allow a mature Christian to plant a new Church, on condition that it is in the nature/likeness of the mother Church. The parent church retains control of the plant, sometimes supporting it financially. But the newly planted church is often no more than an extension of its 'mother', conforming to its nature/likeness. In a sense, this is inevitable. After all, our children display the characteristics they have inherited from us as parents. Nonetheless, a true church plant should have its own identity in Christ, as our children develop their own identities as they grow and leave home. It is also common for the Mother Church to receive tithes from the new plant to emphasise the nature of the relationship. There is rarely release from control. (This is not always the case and there have been many new Churches started on a different basis but, sadly, this is not the norm).

How different this is from the picture of a Sower scattering seed. The Sower does not have a bag of mature plants to sow. No, the Sower sows seeds that carry the DNA of the mature plant. The seeds will grow according to their DNA and become fit for the environment in which they have been planted as they are fed and watered.

God wants us to scatter. The early Church stayed in Jerusalem, seemingly against the express desire of Jesus - so God allowed persecution, which caused great and fast scattering. The result was that the kingdom of God spread rapidly - not just through mature people but also through immature. In fact, the mature people seemed to stay on in Jerusalem.

Today, the most fruitful people carrying the gift of evangelism are new Christians, not mature ones. New Christians burst with the joy of their salvation. They talk - they want to talk, they need to talk - to friends and families, with many positive results. The mature Christians rarely have friends outside the kingdom of God because they do not have the time to find them.

1.8 Confusion and division

God looked at the Tower of Babel and was not pleased. He is not pleased with the Babylonian buildings of today either. The obvious examples are the governments and nations of the world where ungodliness is rampant. Some argue that Babylon is a specific nation or group of nations such as the European Community. But the truth is that the character of Babylon is in all nations, and has become an intricate part of the organised Church.

God's response to the Tower of Babel was to send confusion. He divided their language into many separate tongues so that they were unable to communicate. They lived in confusion.

In Acts 2:8-11 we read that on the day of Pentecost God created clarity out of confusion by sending the gift of tongues. Until Pentecost, languages had been a barrier between different nations. After Pentecost, God gave the gift of tongues and 3000 people from different nations were able to hear God at the same time, clearly. If a man had been in control, he would have had one tongue, with an interpreter. And the difficulty with this is that however good the interpreter the nuances of what is being said may be lost in translation. In addition, everyone is asked to conform to the same message. God, however, had - and has - many tongues with many messages. He speaks to each one of us who is willing to listen in the language, both actual and spiritual, which we can understand bringing clarity and a deeper relationship with Him. I do not know how Peter managed to speak to the same people with his message in Acts 2: 14-40 immediately afterwards - perhaps those present interpreted this one into many languages.

Yet, three hundred years later a new "Babylon" had been built in the name of God. A huge organisation, controlled by man and for man's benefit. The Roman Caesar, Constantine, proclaimed "Christianity" to be the main religion in the Roman Empire having shaped it to his own design. In short, a Babylonian church.

Again, God looked at it and was not pleased. He dealt with it by sending confusion - as He did when the first Tower of Babel was built. This time the confusion was in the form of doctrine – more pernicious because it spread, directed, throughout the then known world. Doctrine is man's attempt to define God and His ways. It was then – it is now - an attempt to put God into an understandable and controllable form. The outcome is plain for everyone to see; each new doctrine results in a new division. A new division resulting in separation. A separation evidenced today in a multitude of doctrines, thousands of divided Churches, throughout the world.

The character of Babylon can be seen everywhere. The call of the Holy Spirit is for God's people to come out of her.

2.0 Babylon's war against Israel

2.1 Initial territorial battles

In Genesis 14:1-16 we read, "About this time war broke out in the region. King Amraphel of Babylonia, King Arioch of Ellasar, King Kedorlaomer of Elam, and King Tidal of Goiim fought against King Bera of Sodom, King Birsha of Gomorrah, King Shinab of Admah, King Shemeber of Zeboiim, and the king of Bela (also called Zoar). This second group of kings joined forces in Siddim Valley (that is, the valley of the Dead Sea). For twelve years they had been subject to King Kedorlaomer, but in the thirteenth year they rebelled against him.

One year later Kedorlaomer and his allies arrived and defeated the Rephaites at Ashteroth-karnaim, the Zuzites at Ham, the Emites at Shaveh-kiriathaim, and the Horites at Mount Seir, as far as El-paran at the edge of the wilderness. Then they turned back, and came to En-mishpat (now called Kadesh) and conquered all the territory of the Amalekites, and the Amorites living in Hazazon-tamar.

Then the rebel kings of Sodom, Gomorrah, Admah, Zeboiim, and Bela (also called Zoar) prepared for battle in the valley of the Dead Sea. They fought against King Kedorlaomer of Elam, King Tidal of Goiim, King Amraphel of Babylonia, and King Arioch of Ellasar—four kings against five. As it happened, the valley of the Dead Sea was filled with tar pits. And as the army of the kings of Sodom and Gomorrah fled, some fell into the tar pits, while the rest escaped into the mountains. The victorious invaders then plundered Sodom and Gomorrah and headed for home, taking with them all the spoils of war and the food supplies. They also captured Lot—Abram's nephew who lived in Sodom—and carried off everything he owned. But one of Lot's men escaped and reported everything to Abram the Hebrew, who was living near the oak grove belonging to Mamre the Amorite. Mamre and his relatives, Eshcol and Aner, were Abram's allies.

When Abram heard that his nephew Lot had been captured, he mobilized the 318 trained men who had been born into his household. Then he pursued

Kedorlaomer's army until he caught up with them at Dan. There he divided his men and attacked during the night. Kedorlaomer's army fled, but Abram chased them as far as Hobah, north of Damascus. Abram recovered all the goods that had been taken, and he brought back his nephew Lot with his possessions and all the women and other captives."

We saw that Nimrod, a hunter/warrior had a vision to build an empire, and built Babylon. That empire started as a series of hill forts. From those he subdued the people living in the region, building a reputation as a cruel warrior as he did. We do not know whether he fulfilled his dream or died before he obtained an empire. But he laid a foundation on which later generations built, Babylon becoming a major world super power in its day.

In Genesis 14, we find the empire vision within Babylon taking root with the first recorded battle of the region enacted as the kings of Sodom, Gomorrah, Admah, Zeboiim, and Bela rebel against the kings of Babylonia, Elam, and Goiim. For 12 years, Babylon and her allies had forced these kings to submit to her authority; the time had come for them to rebel. However, the battle did not go well for the rebels. The kings of Babylonia, Elam, and Goiim captured Abraham's nephew, Lot, who lived in Sodom. As a result, Abraham decided to rescue him.

Perhaps this story illustrates how God's people should relate to the world in which they live; a world that contains many opposing forces. Abraham is not immediately involved in the conflict. Even though he lived in the area, he was not an active member within the tribes caught up in the events. He did not become involved until the kings took his nephew prisoner; then Abraham became the rescuer. He mobilised his household guard and defeated the kings who had opposed the kings of his region.

God calls His people today to be separate from the world and not to be mixed with it. We should be "in" the world but not "of" it; people who are travelling through with a home in a different country. God calls us to be citizens of heaven, not of earth, with our hearts, minds, and expectations in heaven's ruler, Jesus. Abraham seems to have had this attitude. He did not become mixed with the world's battle until he went to rescue Lot. It was not his battle. He was walking with God who had previously promised the land to him and his descendants. As far as he was concerned, the tribes living in the region were on borrowed time. He may have seen what was happening as God's way of dealing with them so that the inheritance would become his. Abraham does not disclose his thoughts to us at this time; we can only imagine what was going through his mind. Nonetheless, whatever his thoughts, Abraham did not want to be involved, and was not involved, until he came to Lot's rescue.

Today, leaders of the Christian church encourage people to be involved in all aspects of the world, to take responsibility as much as possible. This is wise counsel but, often, Christians respond by immersing themselves in the culture of the world instead of offering the one true alternative, namely Jesus. In fact many Christians immerse themselves to such an extent that they become "of" the world as well as in her, resorting to using the same techniques the world uses to obtain and maintain power. Christianity has often become a political force instead of a spiritual one. In doing so, it has lost the character of the kingdom of God. In contrast, Abraham was always separate from the people of the region. He did not own land, obtain wives for his children from them, or become involved in their customs and religions. Instead, he chose to be different, unique, as he followed God. Too often today, Christians tend to want to blend into the world instead of being distinct from her.

In Genesis 14, we see the first skirmish in the long war between Babylon and the people of God. At Babel, we saw Babylon in defiance of God rebelling against God's rule. As the spirit of Babylon recovered from the initial defeat at God's hands by the confusion of language, we see her once again seeking to build an empire. But, instead of directly opposing God, she is bringing tribes under her dominion. Once again, God steps in to stand against Babylon, this time using His man, Abraham.

Throughout history, God has opposed the spirit of Babylon and empire building. Sometimes He has done so by direct opposition; sometimes by using His people.

And sometimes by using an ungodly people - because His people were not available, having strayed from Him.

The events of Genesis 14 are instructive in seeing how Babylon works and what she wants. She works using oppression and control. She wants dominion and wealth. We see these characteristics in many places today. Sales people use these methods to obtain business. They will telephone a potential customer, spin a story about a possible crisis waiting to happen, in order to create fear, which will bring the potential customer under their control, and create an imaginary need and desire to obtain the product on sale. Political parties will spin news to create fear that their opponents are incompetent so that they can bring the electorate under their control. Nations go to war in ways that are more brazen, often to obtain dominion and wealth. Sadly, the church uses the same techniques. Speakers seek to control by creating fear in their audience. Perhaps it is fear of the "end times" and what may occur, or of the wrath of God visiting someone who has not tithed. Whatever the reason, it is the spirit of Babylon at work.

Abraham was a stranger to this world and to Babylon. He entered the scene in order to rescue Lot and, having fulfilled his mission, he becomes a stranger again. The tribes, within whose land he lived, respected him and he did much to bless them. But he did not become one of them.

2.2 Babylon's temptation

Babylon grew to become a major world force dominating much of the Middle East, but during its early years, it was also a centre for trade. We find in Joshua 7:21 that the people of Babylon made beautiful robes and these were traded with the peoples of the Promised Land. They were so beautiful that Achan was willing to disobey God and steal them. That resulted in the loss of many lives, and defeat for the army of Israel in their attempt to dislodge the people of Ai. In Joshua's after-battle investigation, Achan confesses, *"Among the plunder I saw a beautiful robe from Babylon, 200 silver coins, and a bar of gold weighing more than a pound. I wanted them so much that I took them. They are hidden in the ground beneath my tent, with the silver buried deeper than the rest." (NLT)*

The material goods of "spiritual" Babylon still tempt the people of God. Many, not realising the fullness of the kingdom of God, have said that they will wait until they are old before "becoming a Christian" in order to enjoy the sin of the world. Many die before knowing Jesus and His gift of real life. Most waste their lives with things that will be burnt on the Day of Judgement. But, the temptation is real and powerful to the extent that many are taken in by the empty beauty that is on offer.

A robe tempted Achan. It sounds a minor thing in itself so why was he tempted to steal it along with 20 pieces of silver and a gold bar - especially when the Israelites had travelled through the desert for 40 years having no need for money or clothes. And, why were the consequences so severe? In the desert, God gave them manna for their food and they had their animals for clothes. Their shoes did not wear out. God had supplied all he needed throughout Achan's life. But now he is tested over a robe, coins, and bar of gold.

Perhaps Achan had never been satisfied with God's provision. Perhaps he considered it too meagre, as did the majority of the Israelites. Perhaps he thought he deserved something better. We are not told the reason he stole these things. But we do know the consequences were that the army of Israel was defeated. God saw Achan's greed and judged it. Judged it as if the whole nation had sinned (Joshua 7:1) which some may think unduly harsh. Yet God found it to be necessary; a discipline to bring home to His people the need for them to follow Him wholeheartedly if they were to have His blessings.

Having said that, God does not deal with mankind in the same way today. We stand before Him for our own sins rather than the sins of others. When Ananias and Sapphira lied to God in the early days of the Church (Acts 5), God judged them individually. He did not harm the rest of His people.

Achan saw a beautiful robe from Babylon. A robe of this sort covers the body to enhance its beauty or hide the blemishes. It is designed to make the wearer look attractive. Achan wanted to cover himself, or someone else to make them look better than they really were. We can see the subtle temptation of pride in this robe. Pride makes us want to rise up.

The temptations of Babylon are everywhere; particularly in the western throwaway society. A common temptation is to be dissatisfied with what we have and to want more; to make ourselves look better than what we really are. We are willing to carry huge debt in order to buy things that satisfy our temptation rather than be satisfied with what we have and to trust God for more.

A Babylonian robe is a picture of the way we cover over those parts of our lives that are ugly, to make ourselves look better than reality. When Adam and Eve sinned in the Garden of Eden they suddenly realised they were naked and covered themselves with leaves. They were unhappy with what they really were. God's answer was not leaves that quickly perished and would need replacing - a picture of our inability to cover our sinful nature. His answer was to kill a lamb and use the skin for clothes - a picture of the way Jesus was sacrificed and now covers us, freeing us from sin forever.

We see many "Babylonian robes" in our society. Depressed people take a "happy pill" to make them appear different to what they really are without dealing with the root cause for the depression. Obese people have surgery to cut out unwanted flesh. Excitement is found in fast cars; confidence is found in facial make up and clothes. There are many Babylonian temptations, none of which help to deal with the emptiness of the person who succumbs.

The church also contains her Babylonian temptations. The lure of leadership in order to be recognised and obtain power is a common temptation. But perhaps the need for acceptance from a peer group is even more common. A group can cover a person like a robe, giving certain standards and rules that may be met without the need for a changed life. The group member has acceptance without the need for change. Acceptance which covers that person's real need – the need for that man, that woman, to walk with God's Spirit.

God did not let Achan sin without bringing it to the surface and dealing with it. He desired purity in His people and purged out the sin. Today, He still requires purity - and Jesus came to earth to become the way for us to obtain that purity through total cleansing. If we do not accept the Way, we remain in Babylon.

The severity of the treatment towards Achan for this theft – the death of Achan and his family – seems extreme from today's perspective. However, we live in a different age where different spiritual rules apply. In Achan's time, many centuries before the arrival of Jesus, as God's chosen nation, Israel was called to demonstrate His kingdom and life style. God gave them His law for guidance and expected total obedience to His word, given through anointed people. He dealt with the nation rather than individuals. Nonetheless, an individual's sin - Achan's sin - as Adam's before him had an impact on the nation. It resulted in national disgrace and loss. In order to remove the cancer of sin, to restore the nation to Him, God cut out the sinful man and his possessions.

God does not deal with us in this way today. When Jesus came 2000 years ago, He changed the way God interacts with mankind. Jesus did this by fulfilling the demands of the law, and by enabling us to relate to God on an individual basis through Him. As Jesus explained, He is the Way, the Truth, and the Life; no one can come to God except through Him. No longer is it a national relationship: now it is an individual one. We individually walk with God but become part of a nation/kingdom of people who also walk with Him through faith in Jesus and not through physical birth. As a result, God calls us out of Babylon on an individual basis. And we have to respond individually. We cannot depend on someone else to make decisions that only we can make.

A beautiful robe from Babylon caused national disgrace to Israel. Are we prepared to make different choices to that of Achan in our generation?

2.3 Babylon's strategy

Babylon does not seem to crop up in Israel's history after Achan's temptation until the time God allowed them to go into captivity many years later. Israel became a great nation through the exploits of David as he followed God and overcame the enemies surrounding him. But then Israel lost this greatness as the kingdom divided. King after king followed strange gods, worshipped idols, and took part in despicable practices. Eventually, God allowed the King of Assyria to invade Israel and her people were taken captive, exiled in Assyria. Israel had become an ungodly nation. The Israelites were being punished by God. Yet He still wanted her as His people.

Israel's decline started from the time that Jereboam rebelled against Rehoboam, Solomon's son and preferred leader after his death. Jereboam lead the rebellion and then crafted a golden calf as an idol for Israel to worship; an idol to stop them from visiting Jerusalem, in case they decided to form an alliance with Judah against him. After that, Israel followed many gods, drifted away from true worship, until God left them to the mercy of the King of Assyria.

The tribe of Judah had not yet sunk to the levels of depravity of Israel and God allowed them to remain in their territory for a while longer.

We read in 2 Kings 17:24 (NLT) *"The king of Assyria transported groups of people from Babylon, Cuthah, Avva, Hamath, and Sepharvaim and resettled them in the towns of Samaria, replacing the people of Israel. They took possession of Samaria and lived in its towns."* Foreign people, including Babylonians, settled in the promised land of Israel and brought their foreign gods with them.

God may have allowed this settlement but He was not happy with the introduction of foreign gods into His territory and sent lions to wake them to His ownership. This resulted in the people realising they needed to find out how to worship the God of this territory and they found a priest to teach them. However, at the same time, they worshipped their other gods (v29-32) and we see a land with a mixture of worship to God and gods. *"But these various groups of foreigners also continued to worship their own gods. In town after town where they lived, they placed their idols at the pagan shrines that the people of Samaria had built. Those from Babylon worshiped idols of their god Succoth-benoth. Those from Cuthah worshipped their god Nergal. And those from Hamath worshiped Ashima. The Avvites worshipped their gods Nibhaz and Tartak. And the people from Sepharvaim even burned their own children as sacrifices to their gods Adrammelech and Anammelech. These new residents worshipped the Lord, but they also appointed from among themselves all sorts of people as priests to offer sacrifices at their places of worship."*

How did Israel become so empty of God that Babylon could find a place within her? It is interesting that Babylon enters Israel at the invitation of Assyria and not because of a full frontal attack. That came later against Judah. Babylon comes to settle because Israel opened her doors to every strange god that enticed her. God instructed Israel to have Him as the one true God and to remain faithful to Him. Instead, Israel worshipped many gods, following the demonic practices of those gods such as child sacrifice, until their true God released them to their folly. God's promise to her was that Israel would be the head and not the tail if they followed Him. But they forfeited this promise by their actions. They became the tail as their land fell to the domination of Assyria and God gave it to other tribes, including Babylon.

The world today boasts of many religions. Christianity is the largest with 2.2 billion adherents. Few of this number walk with God and, in many instances, their religion is the result of birth not choice. It follows that few of this number are really God's people as there is no relationship with Him.

It was the same in Israel before Assyria captured the territory and people. Many called themselves Israel, but few followed God. The result was He allowed them to go into captivity. Just because we call ourselves Christian, does not provide God's protection. He will allow many disasters to overtake the nations in order for them to come to an awareness of Him. The West, which calls itself Christian, suffers with pride and arrogance because of the past blessings of God. It will take very little to destroy the wealth and prominence of those in the West when their time has come.

Israel turned her back on God and was taken into captivity. Their land was given to Babylon and others who brought mixture and impurity. And this is what Babylon always brings - mixture and impurity. We see the same pattern today as Babylon has mixed with the church. Babylon has brought her own idols. The pinnacle of this probably came with Constantine in 300AD. Much has been written about Constantine and the way he brought Christianity to become the state recognised Church. Some applaud him for what he did but most see his actions as self-motivated and disingenuous. History tells us that he merged his worship of the sun with Christianity to produce a religion that all parts of the empire would accept. In doing so, he made a religion that included all gods, changing the names of the Christian God to become the same as those of the Roman ones. The sun became a prominent part of formal

Christian worship and the day of worship became the sun's day.

Constantine seemed to have no experience of true worship and walk with God. By the time he became aware of Christianity, the original followers of Jesus were long gone to their reward. The Church had drifted from walking with God to formalised meetings and structured services. Constantine would not have seen much of the true life of the Holy Spirit in God's people. What he saw he was able to manipulate to become a state religion, controlled by the state, with new rules and procedures that glorified man and ignored the voice of God.

The same situation exists today. Many people have been involved with the formal institution of the Church but have not much experience of the life of God within people. They have brought much that is ungodly into the Church's practice. An example of this is the way that the Church relies on psychology in their pastoral counselling rather than the Holy Spirit. Most Churches do not allow anyone to counsel others unless they have a formal qualification. And this qualification is more important to them than the fact of someone who is walking with the Holy Spirit. Of course, it is important that vulnerable people are protected and not exposed to immature control freaks or the more outlandish element of Christianity. But, surely, someone who has been walking with God and able to hear the Holy Spirit is preferable to someone with just a secular qualification?

When Babylon took Israel into captivity, the nation lost its identity. The Israelites became immersed in the nations where they were sent. The identity of Israel came to be found in Judah, still living in Jerusalem, and in Benjamin. As foreign tribes settled in Israel the importance of Jerusalem and Judah as the home of the people of God grew. When Judah finally drifted into the worship of foreign gods, God allowed her to become captive for 70 years after which He allowed the nation to return to Jerusalem and Judah. Israel never did return as a nation other than in part when Judah returned. I think the message here is that God is waiting for a people who are whole-hearted for Him. He does not want mixture - and He will not accept lukewarmness.

2.4 The open Door for Babylon

In 2 Kings 23:26-27 we read " *Nevertheless, the LORD did not turn away from the heat of his fierce anger, which burned against Judah because of all that Manasseh had done to provoke him to anger. So the LORD said, "I will remove Judah also from my presence as I removed Israel, and I will reject Jerusalem, the city I chose, and this temple, about which I said, 'There shall my Name be."*

Despite seeing the consequences of sin in the fate of the nation of Israel, Judah also sinned against the Lord. Judah had some godly kings but, sadly, she also had ungodly ones and these kings turned the people against God. Finally, King Jehoahaz came to the throne and in doing evil opened the door to Pharaoh Neco to plunder Judah's gold and silver and take the nation captive to Egypt. His brother, Jehoiakim, ruled over Judah in his place.

Jehoiakim was ungodly. 2 Kings 24:1-4 tells us that during his reign, King Nebuchadnezzar of Babylon invaded Judah and God fulfilled His promise to destroy this tribe also. Judah's kings continued to worship other gods and finally Babylon took the nation into captivity. Every important building in Jerusalem was burned down, and the Temple was destroyed (2 Kings 25:1-8).

Judah had not always been an ungodly nation. 2 Kings 20:12-19 tells us that Hezekiah had been a godly king removing the pagan shrines and turning the nation back to God. He had a miraculous healing during which the Lord caused time to go backwards. He knew God's protection in many ways. Nonetheless, he also allowed Babylon entrance into the nation. As a direct consequence, God promises Hezekiah that Babylon will take Judah into captivity.

Babylon is God's tool to judge His people. Although an ungodly nation, God used her to show His people how far they had fallen from Him. It was the case in God's promise to King Hezekiah and it is the same in our day. Hezekiah made the mistake of inviting Babylon to inspect his treasury and all he possessed. He welcomed

Babylon into his domain, and Babylon liked what was on offer.

Hezekiah may have been flattered by receiving a message from the King of Babylon; this may be the reason for welcoming him to inspect his treasures. Babylon was the up and coming nation and Hezekiah may not have wanted to offend. But what is clear is that Hezekiah was proud of his treasures and wanted to show them off. Pride was his downfall.

It is strange that such a good king who led a spiritual revival and sought the Lord should be the person to open the door for Babylon. Perhaps God, knowing the kings to come and judging the nation over many years, simply used Hezekiah's actions as an opportunity to prophesy the downfall of the nation and it was not a judgement on Hezekiah. It was his pride in his achievements and treasures, though, that gave the opportunity and opened the door to Babylon to see what was on offer.

This scenario has been repeated many times in history. God blesses - and people become proud because of the blessing. The consequent pride causes them to flaunt their treasures and Babylon takes possession. We do not seem to learn the lesson of humility. Church history has many similar examples of the cycle of revival, pride, and loss. The Holy Spirit comes to bring peoples and nations back to God, only for man to create positions of authority and structures of control in which Babylon eventually dominates. Pride is a magnetic force that attracts Babylon; it is in the very character of Babylon.

When the Babylonian influence comes in, the result is domination and the resettlement of the people of God. They are taken out of their land and replaced with foreigners. On the positive side, new people come in and are exposed to the Spirit of God in His land. But what example are they exposed to? Man has created a model that is dominated by man; a model that has little resemblance to the Kingdom of God.

Consider the models of the church or Kingdom on show in the world today. What do we see? Jesus prayed that the world would see unity in the same way as He and His Father were united (John17) and that they would see love amongst the people. "*After saying all these things, Jesus looked up to heaven and said, "Father, the hour has come. Glorify your Son so he can give glory back to you. For you have given him authority over everyone. He gives eternal life to each one you have given him. And this is the way to have eternal life — to know you, the only true God, and Jesus Christ, the one you sent to earth. I brought glory to you here on earth by completing the work you gave me to do. Now, Father, bring me into the glory we shared before the world began.*

"I have revealed you to the ones you gave me from this world. They were always yours. You gave them to me, and they have kept your word. Now they know that everything I have is a gift from you, for I have passed on to them the message you gave me. They accepted it and know that I came from you, and they believe you sent me.

"My prayer is not for the world, but for those you have given me, because they belong to you. All who are mine belong to you, and you have given them to me, so they bring me glory. Now I am departing from the world; they

are staying in this world, but I am coming to you. Holy Father, you have given me your name; now protect them by the power of your name so that they will be united just as we are. During my time here, I protected them by the power of the name you gave me. I guarded them so that not one was lost, except the one headed for destruction, as the Scriptures foretold.

"Now I am coming to you. I told them many things while I was with them in this world so they would be filled with my joy. I have given them your word. And the world hates them because they do not belong to the world, just as I do not belong to the world. I'm not asking you to take them out of the world, but to keep them safe from the evil one. They do not belong to this world any more than I do. Make them holy by your truth; teach them your word, which is truth. 18 Just as you sent me into the world, I am sending them into the world. And I give myself as a holy sacrifice for them so they can be made holy by your truth.

"I am praying not only for these disciples but also for all who will ever believe in me through their message. I

pray that they will all be one, just as you and I are one—as you are in me, Father, and I am in you. And may they be in us so that the world will believe you sent me.

"I have given them the glory you gave me, so they may be one as we are one. I am in them and you are in me. May they experience such perfect unity that the world will know that you sent me and that you love them as much as you love me. Father, I want these whom you have given me to be with me where I am. Then they can see all the glory you gave me because you loved me even before the world began!

"O righteous Father, the world doesn't know you, but I do; and these disciples know you sent me. I have revealed you to them, and I will continue to do so. Then your love for me will be in them, and I will be in them.""

He expected us to demonstrate His Kingdom. A Kingdom where miracles and healing are a daily occurrence. Instead, the models of the church today show that we have opened the door to Babylon. We demonstrate domination, enmity, powerlessness; a dependence on the services of the world for health and finance. There are occasional miracles and acts of kindness, but they are not the main demonstration of the people of God today. I am not saying that we should not use the services of the world but we should not be dependent on them.

Babylon resettles people. Many churches resettle people on a regular basis. Sometimes resettlement occurs because church members do not agree with doctrine or a personality and leaders ask them to find a different church. Often, a church divides into small groups, selected by the leadership. Settlement takes place as the groups are organised but after a time it often happens that the leaders decide some of the groups are not working properly and the members of that group are moved.

This is re-settlement.

The character of Babylon is everywhere in the churches. We are blind to it as was Hezekiah when he invited Babylon to look at his treasures. We desperately need to ask the Holy Spirit to open our eyes so that we might see what He sees.

3.0 Babylon and the Church in the New Testament

The relationship of Babylon and Israel with Jerusalem takes up a large amount of the Old Testament. Some books prophesy the coming of Babylon, others recount the overthrow of Israel, others the history in captivity. Babylon is an important subject of the Old Testament and a clear warning for God's people today.

In the New Testament, national domination has moved on. When it was written Rome was now the power of the day, Babylon and the Babylonian character were not the dominant themes, although they were there, in the background as it were. Nonetheless, in the book of Revelation John receives visions and warnings that again have Babylon as the central figure and Babylon becomes the city that is finally overthrown to usher in the Kingdom of God.

John was writing during a time of fierce persecution from Rome. He may have been using the name "Babylon" as a synonym for Rome. More probably, he was using the word as a spiritual picture, to describe the enemy at war with God's people from the beginning, both physically and spiritually and it is natural for God to explain how this war will finish. It is possible that John did not know the importance of or understand what he was writing. Like Daniel before him, John is writing things that will be understood when the right time has arrived, or when they have been fulfilled.

In what we now call the "Book of Revelation", is a letter written to 7 city networks of Christians in the province of Asia. (Revelation 1 to 4) The content of this letter is both specific to the individual networks (we will call them churches) in the first three chapters and general to the whole world from chapter 4 onwards. In each letter to a church, God gives the promise of a specific reward. A reward to those who overcome the particular difficulty of that church, and a general call to anyone who has ears to hear what the Holy Spirit is saying.

People often interpret the book of Revelation solely as a vision of events of the future, and it does contain much material about these things. But the main purpose of the book is to reveal Jesus and the people who are with Him forever. The book reveals the judgement of God on those who reject Jesus as well as offering promises to those who are faithful to Him. The first chapters are about the church's relationship to Him. After many warnings to the church, Jesus addresses the world then - and now- telling of the fate awaiting those who do not repent, and concluding by describing the end of Satan. After the judgement of Satan, the New Jerusalem comes down from heaven to earth and the culmination of all things take place.

In the letters written to seven Churches existing at the time, we can see the underlying development of the Babylonian character. The door of welcome to God from the church is closing until, finally, we find Jesus outside, knocking at the door. Knocking at the door and patiently asking for entrance so that He and Father can enjoy fellowship together with those in the church. The Babylonian character closes the door to God; it is only when that character has been defeated that fellowship can be restored.

Chapter 1: 9 → gives an introduction of Jesus as the One standing in the middle of the Churches holding the source of revelation and judgement, revealing His character to each Church differently.

3.1 Ephesus

The first letter is to Ephesus (Rev 2:1-7) introducing Jesus - the One who holds the Church there, and the angel there, in His hands – as He does all the churches and angels He writes to, angels being messengers who bring God's word or revelation to the earth.

""Write this letter to the angel of the church in Ephesus. This is the message from the one who holds the seven stars in his right hand, the one who walks among the seven gold lamp stands: "I know all the things you do. I have seen your hard work and your patient endurance. I know you don't tolerate evil people. You have examined the claims of those who say they are apostles but are not. You have discovered they are liars. You have patiently suffered for me without quitting. "But I have this complaint against you. You don't love me or each other as you did at first! Look how far you have fallen! Turn back to me and do the works you did at first. If you don't

repent, I will come and remove your lampstand from its place among the churches. But this is in your favor: You hate the evil deeds of the Nicolaitans, just as I do. "Anyone with ears to hear must listen to the Spirit and understand what he is saying to the churches. To everyone who is victorious I will give fruit from the tree of life in the paradise of God."

Initially Jesus seems to commend the people of God in Ephesus for their hard work and patient endurance for not tolerating evil people and for exposing false apostles. But it becomes obvious that this is not really commendation: the actions were done out of the wrong spirit. They have lost their first love and what they are doing is done out of legalism, not love. The one commendation is that they hated the deeds of the immoral Nicolaitans.

We can clearly see the character of Babylon in this group of people. When considering the Tower of Babel I highlighted eight aspects of the character of Babylon. These are settling, plain dwelling, city builders, made of bricks, requiring asphalt for cement, wanting a name (pride), becoming static, and confusion.

In Ephesus, they worked hard - yet without the Spirit of God. They were obsessed with doctrine and religion. This shows they were settling, living on the plain, made of bricks, and requiring asphalt for adhesion. To their credit, the Nicolaitans had not yet seduced them, even though they were clearly on the scene. Nicolaitans were rulers of the people. They had given themselves positions of rulership over others and created hierarchy. The church in Ephesus was still meeting without hierarchy so they were following the original practices - but without the life of the Spirit that made this worthwhile.

The encouragement given to this group of people is that if they are victorious they will eat from the tree of life in the paradise of God. They needed life immediately in order to return to their first love: if they found that life, they would continue to eat from the tree in paradise. The meaning of the word paradise, as with many words, has been corrupted to mean something different from its original purpose - a description of our life with God after we physically die. If we find real life now we will enjoy eating from the source of life forever. Today, paradise is a word used to mean anything that is comfortable. If a tired person sits in a chair, he or she may well say, "This is paradise". It is also used as a term to explain a mythical place. The emphasis has been taken away from life with God to things of comfort.

Jesus still embraces this group of people, although they are living out of legalism and not life. He does not reject them yet, but gives a warning - they will not find fulfilment in the Kingdom of God unless they repent and find real life. If they continue with a Babylonian character, they will have their lamp stand taken away.

There are many ways that different people have interpreted this passage. Some say it relates only to a church of John's time; others say that these letters show the historical development of the Church through all ages; yet others consider the character of each church as being typical of all churches and that the purpose of the letters is to describe different churches today. There is probably truth in all interpretations. But I see the development of Babylon - with a warning to us that we must extricate ourselves from the Babylonian character or we will lose our lamp stand of testimony. All these churches in Revelation lost their lamp stand because they did not heed the warning. Within a relatively short period, these churches became extinct.

3.2 Smyrna

The next letter is to God's people in Smyrna. We see deterioration in the relationship with God of "those who called themselves Jews, but were not" and an acceptance by them of the "wanting a name" - a character of Babylon. The church was dividing as arguments rose.

"Write this letter to the angel of the church in Smyrna. This is the message from the one who is the First and the Last, who was dead but is now alive: "I know about your suffering and your poverty—but you are rich! I know the blasphemy of those opposing you. They say they are Jews, but they are not, because their synagogue belongs to Satan. Don't be afraid of what you are about to suffer.

The devil will throw some of you into prison to test you. You will suffer for ten days. But if you remain faithful even when facing death, I will give you the crown of life. "Anyone with ears to hear must listen to the Spirit and understand what he is saying to the churches. Whoever is victorious will not be harmed by the second death."

Smyrna means bitterness. Many words have a similar root, including myrrh, a bitter herb. This group faced severe practical and spiritual difficulties. The practical ones were imprisonment and death. The spiritual ones were the increasing growth of deception as pseudo-Christians who claimed to be following God built a foreign religion. John wrote that they called themselves Jews but came from a synagogue of Satan. A synagogue is a religious building used for legalistic and traditional acts of unnecessary "worship". I say unnecessary because the acts of worship, such as the sacrifice of animals, looked forward to a time when the Messiah would arrive whereas He has already come. Their acts of worship spoke of a future death to conquer the power of sin. But Jesus has already completed this sacrifice; there is no need for another death. It is ironic that Smyrna means bitterness. The bitter herb, myrrh, was a gift to Jesus when the wise men visited Him as a child - a sign of the bitterness of His death. Yet parts of the church in Smyrna questioned the value of that death.

The people of God in Smyrna had to contend with a foreign religion whose adherents claimed to be Christian and tried to return to the legalism of the Jews. Ephesus was a place where hierarchy sought to establish the authority of man. Smyrna followed by establishing the religion of man. Much of what takes place in religious buildings today under the guise of being Christian is really of the religion of man. In terms of the character of Babylon, it embraces everything, even confusion.

The promise to those who overcame in Smyrna was that they would escape hurt in the second death. Those who did not overcome did not escape the hurt of the second death.

3.3 Pergamum

As we move on to the letter to Pergamum (Rev 2:12-17) we read this was a city where the House of Satan was located. *"Write this letter to the angel of the church in Pergamum. This is the message from the one with the sharp two-edged sword: "I know that you live in the city where Satan has his throne, yet you have remained loyal to me. You refused to deny me even when Antipas, my faithful witness, was martyred among you there in Satan's city. "But I have a few complaints against you. You tolerate some among you whose teaching is like that of Balaam, who showed Balak how to trip up the people of Israel. He taught them to sin by eating food offered to idols and by committing sexual sin. In a similar way, you have some Nicolaitans among you who follow the same teaching. Repent of your sin, or I will come to you suddenly and fight against them with the sword of my mouth.*

"Anyone with ears to hear must listen to the Spirit and understand what he is saying to the churches. To everyone who is victorious I will give some of the manna

that has been hidden away in heaven. And I will give to each one a white stone, and on the stone will be engraved a new name that no one understands except the one who receives it."

Pergamum was a centre for the worship of Zeus as well as other gods. The people of God remained loyal even though they lived among such opposition. Nonetheless, they allowed the culture access and tolerated people like Balaam and the Nicolaitans. Balaam was a prophet who sold his gift to the highest bidder and, although he seemed to have the ability to hear God, his love of money tempted him to curse God's people. Payment for services from the people of God is common practice nowadays; even to the extent that ministry is seen to be a way to earn a living. It has become a profession rather than a calling, and the example of Balaam is an important warning. He loved money and was willing to go to any lengths to obtain it, even if it involved tripping up the people of God. Throughout the world today, there are many examples of people following the error of Balaam.

Often in Africa, but also elsewhere, religion is seen as a valid way to earn a living. Anyone can start a "church" with no regard to doctrine, faith, or relationship with God. Often, the "church" uses the bible as the text but the practice does not come from God. They allow and encourage multi "marriages" and accept the worship of idols as normal. In more "advanced" countries, the errors of Balaam are more subtle, but they are still present. Ministries increasingly expect payment for Christian activity: Pastors for the provision of counselling; Prophets for "words from God" or worship groups to lead singing. Few expect their provision as a reward from a Heavenly Father for work in His services to be received through faith. Instead, financial reward is expected for any ministry given. The love of money brings its own temptation and, as for Balaam, results in the one ministering fulfilling the desires of the person paying rather than those of the Holy Spirit. In my own experience, I have received requests for a tithe before being allowed to receive any ministry and certain groupings of Churches specifically require a tithe from a Church before they are allowed to join the group.

The Nicolaitans also found a place to expand in this soil at Pergamum. They followed the same sins as Balaam but added the sin of ruling over others. Not satisfied with taking money for services rendered, they also took control over the people making payment. The warning of the Holy Spirit to this Church is that they will find God's sword against the followers of Balaam and the Nicolaitans unless they repent.

It is not my intention to analyse deeply the letters to the Churches in Revelation other than to see the development of the character of Babylon through their history. Here, in the third letter, we see a rapid development as pride takes root. Pride, the raising up above another, enables any error to enter as those leading have the power to introduce whatever they want without fear of reprisal from the people. Babylon's weapon of choice is always pride as this enables anything to become accepted.

It is always possible to avoid the steady incursion of Babylon, but only if we have ears to hear what the Holy Spirit is saying to us. The reward given to those who do hear and respond in Pergamum is twofold: to eat manna hidden in heaven until the time it is needed for sustaining the people of God, and to receive a white stone on which God has written a new name that speaks of the character and purpose of the person concerned. That it is engraved on a white stone speaks of the purity of Jesus. In spite of the difficulty of the time, the persecution, and spiritual decline, it is possible to be within the Body of Christ, and to display His character and purpose.

3.4 Thyatira

The letter to the next Church, Thyatira, opens with an introduction of Jesus as the Son of God whose eyes are bright like flames of fire and whose feet are like polished bronze (Rev 2:18-29). The eyes of Jesus see deeply into our real character, and the fire purifies us, if we respond. His feet, polished until they are a mirror, may speak about the strength that comes from being forged in the furnace. Bronze itself is an alloy of copper and tin used by the Romans for making many items such as statues and coins.

"Write this letter to the angel of the church in Thyatira. This is the message from the Son of God, whose eyes are like flames of fire, whose feet are like polished bronze: "I know all the things you do. I have seen your love, your faith, your service, and your patient endurance. And I can see your constant improvement in all these things. "But I have this complaint against you. You are permitting that woman — that Jezebel who calls herself a prophet — to lead my servants astray. She teaches them to commit sexual sin and to eat food offered to idols. I gave her time to repent, but she does not want to turn away from her immorality. "Therefore, I will throw her on a bed of suffering, and those who commit adultery with her will suffer greatly unless they repent and turn away from her evil deeds. I will strike her children dead. Then all the churches will know that I am the one who searches out the thoughts and intentions of every person. And I will give to each of you whatever you deserve. "But I also have a message for the rest of you in Thyatira who have not followed this false teaching ('deeper truths,' as they call them — depths of Satan, actually). I will ask nothing more of you except

that you hold tightly to what you have until I come. To all who are victorious, who obey me to the very end, to them I will give authority over all the nations. They will rule the nations with an iron rod and smash them like clay pots. They will have the same authority I received from my Father, and I will also give them the morning star! "Anyone with ears to hear must listen to the Spirit and understand what he is saying to the churches."

Jesus sees both good and bad in Thyatira. The good contains love, faith, service, endurance, and continuous improvement. But Jezebel counteracts this. It is not certain whether this is her real name or a label given because of the similarity between this woman and the wife of Ahab. Nonetheless, her actions are clearly stated. She called herself a prophet and many were lead astray by her. The sins of this woman are so blatant, so obviously wrong that it is incredible she could seduce anyone. But at that time and since then, many in every generation have been lead astray by false prophets.

Within living memory there have been two despots responsible for murder on a horrific scale, Stalin in

Russia and Hitler in Germany. Both seduced their nations. Both encouraged mass killings as acceptable, even valuable, acts. Now, in this generation, there are similar atrocities, similar national seduction, somewhere in the world. Sadly, the "church" is seduced along with the rest of the nation. The worship of idols is acceptable practice in many parts of the church and it can be argued that the bible has itself become an object of worship placed above the Living Word. Many Christians take the view that the bible is the last word of God and there is no place for any further word. Such people have great difficulty accepting prophecy – in accepting that God continues to speak to us today. Great difficulty in believing that any other works of the Holy Spirit are as applicable today as they were in the time of Jesus. Other idol worship is of pictures, icons, and even people.

Eating food offered to idols is a strange complaint; Paul and Peter were specifically preaching that this is not a sin. Peter was taught this before meeting Cornelius (Acts 10) and Paul explains the teaching in 1 Cor 8. I believe the problem at Thyatira was a different one. Peter and

Paul dealt with a problem arising through the legalistic and superstitious nature of the Jews; they would not eat meat offered to idols in case it contaminated them. At Thyatira, the people were seeking to find their spiritual nourishment from an idol; they had no concern of contamination; they were already seduced. Their doctrine was evil but they followed it regardless. It is not surprising that they committed sexual sin, often a common development in such circumstances.

Many parts of the Church today accept these sins as normal practice, as they were at the time of this letter, usually through ignorance. The warning from the Son of God is that He will give time for repentance. But, if none is forthcoming, He will judge, causing sickness and death.

Then as now as we trace the development of the character of Babylon, we find a stronghold developing. Then and now many have been lead astray and false doctrine has increased.

3.5 Sardis

The introduction to the letter to the Church in Sardis reveals the character of the writer as "The one who has the sevenfold spirit of God and the seven stars" (Rev 3:1-6). The stars refer to the angels of the Churches and this way of introducing Jesus tells Sardis that they are dealing with the one who holds everything in His hands. They thought they were alive. In fact, they were near death.

"Write this letter to the angel of the church in Sardis. This is the message from the one who has the sevenfold Spirit of God and the seven stars: "I know all the things you do, and that you have a reputation for being alive— but you are dead. Wake up! Strengthen what little remains, for even what is left is almost dead. I find that your actions do not meet the requirements of my God. Go back to what you heard and believed at first; hold to it firmly. Repent and turn to me again. If you don't wake up, I will come to you suddenly, as unexpected as a thief. "Yet there are some in the church in Sardis who have not soiled their clothes with evil.

They will walk with me in white, for they are worthy. All who are victorious will be clothed in white. I will never erase their names from the Book of Life, but I will announce before my Father and his angels that they are mine. "Anyone with ears to hear must listen to the Spirit and understand what he is saying to the churches."

The relationship with God enjoyed by the people of Sardis had deteriorated. They no longer knew how to walk in the Holy Spirit. They were active doing many good works, but these were flesh works, not of the Spirit. The Church today displays much of this character also. There are many good works touching the poor, the sick, and the rejected of society. Worldwide appeals for aid to communities suffering from natural catastrophes such as Tsunami, earthquakes, and volcanoes, as well as manmade disasters of famine and war result in generous contributions from both Church and secular society. Local community projects to provide children's clubs, homes for the homeless, food to the needy and many other activities are all good works. They give the appearance of life, as do lively worship groups and dancing congregations. But, is any of this the life that God is seeking?

Sardis had a reputation for being alive but was near death. True life is the relation of Holy Spirit with man's spirit. It does not require supernatural acts and miracles - although they usually accompany people who are truly alive. True life is itself a supernatural act. We find it, not by an academic awareness of doctrine, or an emotional response to worship, but by the Holy Spirit being Lord of our life.

Activity, whether good or bad, is one of the greatest obstacles to finding God. There is an account in the history of Judah (2 Chron 30) when a good king, Hezekiah, seeks to bring the nation back to God. He restored the Temple and the utensils for worship and decided to hold a Passover feast. This feast eventually lasted two weeks although the original plan was for one. The king wrote to his nation, Judah, and extended the invitation to the then enemy nation of Israel. The Judeans responded in large numbers but Israel did not, most laughing at the idea of wasting time with a feast to a God they had long forgotten. To most of Judah, the feast was a good deed and they came gladly. There is no immediate sense that this was a spiritual response other than a desire to keep the law. To Israel, it was a waste of time; they had other things to do. To the king, it was a spiritual response to the work of God in his life. And by responding as the king and his people did, the Holy Spirit came upon many. Priests came under conviction of their need for purification, as did Levites and common people. The good deed became a time of spiritual revival.

As for Sardis, those in that city had not reached the time of revival. Indeed, as we trace the growth of the character of Babylon we see that Sardis has fallen to a level where pride stopped them seeing how poor they really were. They thought in their pride that they were alive. In fact, they were near death.

3.6 Philadelphia

The next letter is to the church in Philadelphia (Rev 3:7-13). Jesus introduces Himself as the one who is holy and true, holding the keys of David. He opens and shuts doors and no one has the power to contradict what He does.

"Write this letter to the angel of the church in Philadelphia: This is the message from the one who is holy and true, the one who has the key of David. What he opens, no one can close; and what he closes, no one can open: "I know all the things you do, and I have opened a door for you that no one can close. You have little strength, yet you obeyed my word and did not deny me. Look, I will force those who belong to Satan's synago — those liars who say they are Jews but are not — to come and bow down at your feet. They will acknowledge that you are the ones I love. "Because you have obeyed my command to persevere, I will protect you from the great time of testing that will come upon the whole world to test those who belong to this world. I am coming soon. Hold on to what you have, so that no one will take away your crown. All who are victorious will become pillars in the Temple of my God, and they will never have to leave it. And I will write on them the

name of my God, and they will be citizens in the city of my God — the new Jerusalem that comes down from heaven from my God. And I will also write on them my new name. "Anyone with ears to hear must listen to the Spirit and understand what he is saying to the churches."

This introduction of Jesus is comparable to a passage in Isaiah 22:22 where Isaiah also talks about the keys of David. This refers to the highest position in the land of Israel with authority to open and shut doors. Jesus comes to Philadelphia with the promise that the highest possible authority is with them as they follow Him.

We read that the people of God in Philadelphia considered themselves very poor with little strength; but they were obedient; they did not deny Jesus, despite tremendous persecution. It is to this church that Jesus promises an open door.

The scene in this drama is of a small group facing a bleak future with simple trust in their Saviour. There is a "church", that is in error, that belongs to Satan, even though its members confess to be Jews, God's people. That 'church' is creating serious trouble for the Philadelphians: the 'church' probably being a legalistic Jewish sect seeking to bring Christians under the law. The promise is that this pseudo-church will come and bow at the feet of the "weak" group and acknowledge that the love of Jesus is not for them but for the "weak".

There is only one command - to persevere. With perseverance comes the protection of Him who has authority to open and shut doors. With perseverance comes reward.

As we look for Babylon in this city, we find schism, false doctrine and a large group that has banded together for security with no desire to search for the truth or live in right relationship to God. Those in that group are more interested in appearance than in finding reality. The character of Babylon has taken over the people who claim to be of God; they have become a temple of Satan. There are still a few who persevere, but the majority of the people of God are in error.

If we persevere, in spite of having little strength, we find protection from a time of great testing coming to the whole world. This is an enormous promise for people with so little. Even more promise is given, with Jesus offering them the opportunity to be pillars in the Temple and citizens in the New Jerusalem with a new name. The Temple is a description of people, not a building. A pillar is a key part of the construction of a temple, holding up the roof and helping to keep the building together. As we overcome in the situations we live through we reign over the opposition and become strong in the Spirit. By overcoming, we become pillars able to hold up the building God is preparing.

In Philadelphia, we see a picture of the scene today. There are vast numbers in the world who confess to be Christian, to the extent, as I have said earlier, that Christianity is the largest religion. Much that the church teaches and many practices followed, then and now, however, are alien to the ways of God. People who call themselves "Christian" often persecute true Christians – witness, for example, John Bunyan thrown into prison because he was not of the 'established' church and would not give up preaching, or in more recent days, the antagonism between 'charismatic' house churches and established churches. All in all, there seems to be little strength left in the people of God. But as in Philadelphia Jesus promises much to those who persevere.

3.7 Laodicea

In the next letter, to the last church, Laodicea, (Rev 3:14-22) Jesus is introduced as the Amen, the faithful and true witness, the ruler of God's creation. He is permanently and persistently the same. The church is lukewarm and Jesus is ready to spit them out of His mouth. They think they are rich, but have nothing of true value. They rely on money and self-effort rather than the work of God.

"Write this letter to the angel of the church in Laodicea. This is the message from the one who is the Amen — the faithful and true witness, the beginning of God's new creation: "I know all the things you do, that you are neither hot nor cold. I wish that you were one or the other! But since you are like lukewarm water, neither hot

nor cold, I will spit you out of my mouth! You say, 'I am rich. I have everything I want. I don't need a thing!' And you don't realize that you are wretched and miserable and poor and blind and naked. So I advise you to buy gold from me — gold that has been purified by fire. Then you will be rich. Also buy white garments from me so you will not be shamed by your nakedness, and ointment for your eyes so you will be able to see. I correct and discipline everyone I love. So be diligent and turn from your indifference. "Look! I stand at the door and knock. If you hear my voice and open the door, I will come in, and we will share a meal together as friends. Those who are victorious will sit with me on my throne, just as I was victorious and sat with my Father on his throne. "Anyone with ears to hear must listen to the Spirit and understand what he is saying to the churches."

It is easy to see the character of Babylon here. The Laodiceans are building a tower to their own glory and importance. They rely on their wealth (money not spirit) and ability (human not spiritual) to attract people and become large. But the judgement of God is that they need to buy reality from Him. They need gold purified by fire. They need white garments. They need eye salve.

When we are in Christ, we receive freely all the aspects that the Church at Laodicea lacked. We are purified; we are clothed with garments of righteousness; we receive revelation to understand the Spirit of God. Laodicea had nothing of God but much of the soul. There was no fellowship with the Father, Son, and Holy Spirit and we see them standing outside knocking for admittance. It is a tragic picture of the Church. Is this a picture we see fulfilled today?

4.0 The fall of Babylon

Suddenly, with no warning, Revelation 14:8 and 16:9 tells the end of the City of Babylon. There has been no previous mention of the city in Revelation; no warning that one of the main events in history will involve the fall of the city. John does not tell us what Babylon signifies, nor does he give any clues about when this will take place, thus giving rise to many and various opinions. It is not particularly crucial to the purpose of this book to consider this. I am more concerned with the character of Babylon and the need for the people of God to lose this character rather than worrying about the end of Babylon itself. However, I will make a few comments.

In Revelation 17, an angel explains the mystery of Babylon to John.

"One of the seven angels who had poured out the seven bowls came over and spoke to me. " Come with me," he said, "and I will show you the judgment that is going to come on the great prostitute, who rules over many

waters. The kings of the world have committed adultery with her, and the people who belong to this world have been made drunk by the wine of her immorality."

So the angel took me in the Spirit into the wilderness. There I saw a woman sitting on a scarlet beast that had seven heads and ten horns, and blasphemies against God were written all over it. The woman wore purple and scarlet clothing and beautiful jewellery made of gold and precious gems and pearls. In her hand, she held a gold goblet full of obscenities and the impurities of her immorality. A mysterious name was written on her forehead: "Babylon the Great, Mother of All Prostitutes and Obscenities in the World." I could see that she was drunk — drunk with the blood of God's holy people who were witnesses for Jesus. I stared at her in complete amazement. "Why are you so amazed?" the angel asked. "I will tell you the mystery of this woman and of the beast with seven heads and ten horns on which she sits. The beast you saw was once alive but isn't now. And yet he will soon come up out of the bottomless pit and go to eternal destruction. And the people who belong to this world, whose names were not written in the Book of Life before the world was made, will be amazed at the reappearance of this beast who had died. "This calls for a mind with understanding: The seven heads of the beast represent the seven hills where the woman rules. They also represent seven kings. Five kings have already fallen, the sixth now reigns, and the seventh is yet to come, but his reign will be brief.

"The scarlet beast that was, but is no longer, is the eighth king. He is like the other seven, and he, too, is headed for destruction. The ten horns of the beast are ten kings who have not yet risen to power. They will be appointed to their kingdoms for one brief moment to reign with the beast. They will all agree to give him their power and authority. Together they will go to war against the Lamb, but the Lamb will defeat them because he is Lord of all lords and King of all kings. And his called and chosen and faithful ones will be with him."

Then the angel said to me, "The waters where the prostitute is ruling represent masses of people of every nation and language. The scarlet beast and his ten horns *all hate the prostitute. They will strip her naked, eat her flesh, and burn her remains with fire. For God has put a plan into their minds, a plan that will carry out his purposes. They will agree to give their authority to the scarlet beast, and so the words of God* will *be fulfilled. And this woman you saw in your vision represents the great city that rules over the kings of the world."*

The angel describes Babylon as a great prostitute sitting on many waters, ruling the rulers of the world. The Spirit immediately takes John into a wilderness where he sees a woman sitting on a scarlet beast, which has 7 heads and 10 horns and has blasphemies against God written all over. The woman wears purple and scarlet clothing and beautiful jewellery made of gold, precious gems and pearls. In her hand, she holds a gold goblet full of obscenities and the impurities of her immorality. She has a mysterious name written on her forehead: "*Babylon the Great, Mother of All Prostitutes and Obscenities in the World.*" She is drunk — drunk with the blood of God's holy people who were witnesses for Jesus.

Babylon is a mystery, but one which the angel explained. God often gives mysteries. The Church is a mystery that Paul explains as Christ within, the Hope of glory. Colossians 1:27 says, *"To them God has chosen to make known among the Gentiles the glorious riches of this mystery, which is Christ in you, the hope of glory."* Here, in Revelation 17, we have another mystery. In explaining the mystery, the angel starts by describing the beast on which the woman sits demonstrating that she uses the beast to achieve her ends.

In verse 8, we find the beast was once alive but is not now. Yet he will soon come up out of the bottomless pit and go to eternal destruction. The beast has seven heads which represent the seven hills where the woman rules. They also represent seven kings. Five kings have already fallen, the sixth now reigns, and the seventh is yet to come, but his reign will be brief. The scarlet beast that was, but is no longer, is the eighth king. He is like the other seven, and he, too, will be destroyed. This part of the explanation seems to be history now. The kings reigned but have now gone and this is probably a description of the fall of Rome.

The next part of the explanation is for a future time. The angel says, "*The ten horns of the beast are ten kings who have not yet risen to power. They will be appointed to their kingdoms for one brief moment to reign with the beast. They will all agree to give him their power and authority. Together they will go to war against the Lamb, but the Lamb will defeat them because he is Lord of all lords and King of all kings. And his called and chosen and faithful ones will be with him.*"

Just as Satan controlled Rome, he will control ten more kings who will rule at the same time over different countries. They will give Satan authority over their nations and he will take them on a final battle against God.

We have spent a little time looking at the beast but this is not Babylon. Babylon sits on the beast and rules many peoples from every nation and language. Verse 16 says that the scarlet beast and his ten horns all hate the prostitute. They will strip her naked, eat her flesh, and burn her remains with fire, for God has put a plan into their minds, a plan that will carry out his purposes. They will agree to give their authority to the scarlet beast, and so the words of God will be fulfilled.

The angel tells John that Babylon represents the great city that rules over the kings of the world.

Is the Babylon of Revelation a physical city? I think not but many argue it was, is, or will be. It was, at one time, a thriving city and the centre of a mighty nation until it was overthrown and became a wasteland. It remained in this state until, in recent years, Saddam Hussein rebuilt part to become a museum/memorial to his own greatness. Some suggest it will again become a flourishing city and an international centre of trade. I doubt it and do not believe this is what John saw in Revelation.

Some suggest the use of the name Babylon was a way to depict Rome, with the fall of Rome fulfilling the prophecy in Revelation 18. Prophecy often has several depths to its interpretation. It can apply to the time it is given as well as later times; to the people who initially received the word, or to a different people at a later fulfilment. Much of the description of Babylon sitting on a beast in Revelation 17:9 is easily seen in Rome - built on seven hills with a succession of kings or emperors. Rome certainly carried the character of Babylon.

Both Babylon and Jerusalem are physical cities. But both are also spiritual entities and I believe the downfall of Babylon is a picture of the fall of everything ruled by Satan and outside the Kingdom of God. Jerusalem is the city of God, which embraces the people, culture, and authority of His Kingdom. Babylon is Satan's equivalent, which he uses to entice and capture the nations of this world. Physical Jerusalem was built on mountains, as was the physical Babylon seen by John. If Babylon is a physical city dominating the world, it is not yet built. There are many influential cities throughout the world, but none has so much power that the world systems would fall down if it were destroyed.

In recent years, we have seen how the near collapse of major banking and financial businesses in America and Europe threatened destruction so great that in this country the Exchequer has had to shore them up financially. Similar help has had to be given to ailing financial corporations in America, while in Europe members of the European Union have had to come to the rescue. It may not be too fanciful therefore to describe "Banking" as a city!

John sees a physical city because he is in the spirit: he sees spiritual things as if they were physical. This happens in other realms, such as in dreams when unreal events feel as if they are in real life, until we awake. In a similar way, a person seeing a vision sees spiritual things as if they are physical and this is what John is describing.

Babylon, throughout its history, was the destroyer of Israel, as well as any nation that refused to acknowledge its rule. Spiritual Babylon does the same. It obtains rule by bringing people and nations under temptation, by false doctrine, by unwise decisions, by greed. In short, by any means available. Babylon rules anyone who gives it the right to do so.

The end, when it comes, is clearly a work of God. A huge earthquake brings the city down and destroys the nations of the world. The fall of Babylon ushers in the new age of the kingdom of God. We shall look at the character of this kingdom and her people in part two of this book.

5.0 Babylon and John

As we have seen when looking at the book of Revelation, John had an insight into Babylon. In his other letters, John does not mention Babylon by name, but we see the intrusion of the Babylonian character in the church quite clearly.

In 1 John 2: 18-26 we read, *"Dear children, the last hour is here. You have heard that the Antichrist is coming, and already many such antichrists have appeared. From this we know that the last hour has come. These people left our churches, but they never really belonged with us; otherwise they would have stayed with us. When they left, it proved that they did not belong with us. But you are not like that, for the Holy One has given you his Spirit, and all of you know the truth. So I am writing to you not because you don't know the truth but because you know the difference between truth and lies. And who is a liar? Anyone who says that Jesus is not the Christ. Anyone who denies the Father and the Son is an antichrist. Anyone who denies the Son doesn't have the Father, either. But anyone who acknowledges the Son has the Father also. So you must remain faithful to what you have been taught from the beginning. If you do, you will remain in fellowship with the Son and with the Father. And in this fellowship we enjoy the eternal life he promised us.*

I am writing these things to warn you about those who want to lead you astray. But you have received the Holy Spirit, and he lives within you, so you don't need anyone to teach you what is true. For the Spirit teaches you everything you need to know, and what he teaches is true — it is not a lie. So just as he has taught you, remain in fellowship with Christ."

John faced the problems of the early Church. The ultimate judgement on Babylon was that God sent confusion to stop the success of the schemes of the Babylonians. It is the same in John's time. God sends confusion to stop the schemes of the "antichrists". The word *antichrist* means *instead of Christ* rather than *against Christ.* They encouraged people to depend on other things for salvation rather than the work of Jesus on the cross. There were many who sought to lead the early Christians astray, with the ideas of the pagans, or by teaching that Jesus had already returned to earth. John encourages them to reject these ideas and to depend on the Holy Spirit, who was with them and brought unity.

It is the same today. Some Christians emphasise the need for good works in order to find salvation; others, the development of self-ability in order to become a better person. The development of science and human wisdom give many alternatives to the work of the cross to resolve problems. Many Christians prefer these methods to a dependence on the Holy Spirit.

In 1 John 3: 7-10 we read *"Dear children, don't let anyone deceive you about this: When people do what is right, it shows that they are righteous, even as Christ is righteous. But when people keep on sinning, it shows that they belong to the devil, who has been sinning since the beginning. But the Son of God came to destroy the works of the devil. Those who have been born into God's family do not make a practice of sinning, because God's life is in them. So they can't keep on sinning, because they are children of God. So now we can tell who are children of God and who are children of the devil. Anyone who does not live righteously and does not love other believers does not belong to God."*

John highlights a difficulty that the Church faced. There was no difference between the Church and the world in the matter of sin. The Church had lost her "saltiness". John explained that no one who keeps on in the practice of sin is a child of God. Again, we can see the character of Babylon. The people had settled. No longer were they prepared to be pioneers, different from the people around. They were confused as to what it meant to be a child of God.

As we compare this situation with the world today, we see little difference. Go to any part of the Christian world and the statistics show that regions where the Church dominates have the same level of divorce, child lawlessness, violence and all manner of sin as those where there is no Church. The Church is no longer salt and light to the world.

In 3 John v 9, John writes about Diotrephes, a man who loved to be first. Not only did he want pre-eminence, he refused to have anything to do with John and the other Apostles. John does not recognise him or his claim to be pre-eminent. Rather, he judges the actions of Diotrephes to be a bad example.

How often does this situation arise in Churches today? Most churches accept the principle of "first amongst equals" as normal practice. There may be a "team ministry" or "one man ministry" in practice but in either state, it is acceptance of a person or people in pre-eminence. John did not recognise the claims of Diotrephese, nor did he give any indication that someone in pre-eminence was acceptable practice. I have dealt with this issue elsewhere in this book, so will not spend time revisiting it.

6.0 Babylon and Paul

It is no surprise that Paul does not mention Babylon by name. It is only John who does and only then as a title for something else other than a physical place. Paul, being the most prolific writer in the New Testament, and dealing with the problems arising in the early Church, uncovers the character of Babylon in most of his writings. He echoes the call of John in 2 Corinthians 6:14-18: *"Don't team up with those who are unbelievers. How can righteousness be a partner with wickedness? How can light live with darkness? What harmony can there be between Christ and the devil? How can a believer be a partner with an unbeliever? And what union can there be between God's temple and idols? For we are the temple of the living God. As God said: "I will live in them and walk among them. I will be their God, and they will be my people. Therefore, come out from among unbelievers, and separate ourselves from them, says the Lord. Don't touch their filthy things, and I will welcome you. And I will be your Father, and you will be my sons and daughters, says the Lord Almighty."*

Paul saw the same character, as did John and had the same medicine to deal with it – come out of it.

When writing to the Corinthians, Paul addresses the issues of division, pride, immorality, and confusion about a number of topics, He does not give the choice to continue as they are but exhorts them to leave behind these ungodly and unhelpful traits.

In 2 Corinthians 4:2, Paul specifically states that he does not use deception in his preaching, deception being a character trait of Babylon. Paul chose to leave deception behind; he wanted only to give the power of the truth of the Word to his hearers.

To the Romans, Paul writes a letter explaining what Jesus has achieved and how they could enter into the benefits of this. He was addressing people born in the centre of the Roman world and who had imbibed all that Rome offered. We benefit in having such a thorough explanation from him, but he had to write it to show the truth to his hearers. Paul has to show them that they have died to the old way of life and should not be continuing in it.

Wherever we read in Paul's letters, we find that he is addressing a confused people. He encourages them to leave the confusion behind and move into the clarity of the truth of Jesus. Clarity needed today because confusion still reigns: confusion of doctrine, and confusion of allegiance – whether to God or to man.

Paul does not demonstrate the character of Babylon himself. We saw that Nimrod, the architect of Babylon, was an empire builder. He wanted to be the top man in the empire. Paul does not have empire at heart. Instead, he has one ambition – to see the Kingdom of God. He was happy to be nothing, the least of the apostles, and the apostles were the doormats of everyone, in order for the Kingdom of God to become known to everyone. In Philippians 1, Paul says that he was happy to be a prisoner in chains if it enabled the good news of the kingdom to be spread in Rome.

Paul did not settle in the plains of Babylon. Instead, he was constantly seeking for fresh revelation of the plans of God. As we read his letters, we see a progression of revelation as he grew in the Spirit. When he neared his death, Paul said that he had finished his fight and was ready for his reward. He kept pressing forward until he died.

Paul did not build a city or a monument for his own reputation. Rather, he gave everything for the kingdom of God. He did not build a network of churches in competition with others. Instead, he rebuked those who caused division; he encouraged discipline of divisive people. He said to the Corinthians, *"And you should imitate me, just as I imitate Christ."*. He did not want followers; he wanted people to follow Christ.

Unfortunately, there are people today who see Paul as a hierarchical woman hater, believing in titles, positions, and male superiority. This is a misunderstanding - of Paul and of the New Testament. Paul believed in equality of the sexes and the races. We are all one in Christ Jesus with different gifts and abilities but equal before God. We are to submit to each other, not have a leadership structure promoting class differences. Paul did not accept Babylonian practices, nor did he encourage them anywhere.

7.0 Our Response

In Revelation 18:4, the Holy Spirit tells us the response He expects from us. A voice comes from heaven urgently telling the people of God to leave Babylon. Today, at the end of the age, the Holy Spirit is urgently telling us to respond to the warning. The organised church is in Babylon. The character of Babylon is everywhere we look. The practices of Babylon are followed wherever leaders seek to control a group of followers.

The response of leaders to Jesus and His original followers was to reject the message of salvation and ignore the warnings. Today, we have another opportunity. Will we help people, show them the way, to Jerusalem or to Babylon?

It is easier for people who are not official leaders to respond to the warning of the Holy Spirit. They do not have so much to "lose". They do not have the position, reputation, or financial strings holding them back. Instead, they can just leave Babylon.

In places where people have responded to the call to leave Babylon, networks of relationships are growing. These are not house churches or another fixed group. They are relationships formed by the Holy Spirit with the freedom to build with anyone the Holy Spirit chooses. The relationships join a community together and build bridges between different locations. They are an opportunity for God's people to become one under the King Jesus.

Part Two

Jerusalem

Jerusalem

1.0 Introduction

There is a clear distinction between natural and spiritual Jerusalem. We will only consider the natural growth of Jerusalem minimally: spiritual Jerusalem is our main goal. We will look at the people of biblical history and in doing so will consider their character, especially as it reflects on the City of God, the New Jerusalem.

We can see the roots of the City itself in Abraham, and we shall start with him, although we can glean the character of God's people from earlier days as well. We will consider some of these afterwards. Of necessity, the sample will be small.

1.1 Jerusalem - The Roots

Despite God's instruction to Joshua and the people of Israel to take possession of the land when they first entered it (Joshua 1), they did not capture the city of Jerusalem until many generations later. Joshua tried, but we read in Joshua 15:63, that he could not dislodge the Jebusites. In Judges 1:8, we find that Israel takes the city, puts it to the sword, and burns it down. The

Jebusites rebuilt the city and made it into a strong fortress, co-existing with the Israelites for a long time.

King Saul reigned many years without possessing Jerusalem or even giving her any attention. It was not until the time of King David that we find Jerusalem becoming the focus of a godly king. In 1 Chronicles 11 we read that David is made king and immediately he captures Jerusalem, despite the taunts of the Jebusites that he would not be able to do so. The Jebusites were descended from Ham, like Nimrod (Gen 10:6-16). Chronicles is a book about the spiritual journey of Israel. It does not necessarily follow her path chronologically but does highlight the key spiritual aspects. The Holy Spirit knows how important it is that we understand that David captured Jerusalem first. The message from God is clear. Does the spiritual son of Ham possess God's spiritual city now?

Sadly, I believe the answer is "yes". Jesus stated that He gives His people a kingdom - but they have not possessed the city. We have been obsessed with the organisation of the church. We have missed the heart of

God, which is that we become His City. We have lived with a foreign people in our midst, as Israel allowed the Jebusites. We have been disobedient to God's injunction to be a separate people.

Genesis 22 tells us of the beginnings of the events at a mountain called "The Mountain of the Lord". This mountain eventually became synonymous with Jerusalem, and the first purposes of God and man on her show that His intention was that man should build Jerusalem in a different way, and for different motives, to those of Babylon.

"Some time later, God tested Abraham's faith. " Abraham!" God called. "Yes," he replied. "Here I am." "Take your son, your only son — yes, Isaac, whom you love so much — and go to the land of Moriah. Go and sacrifice him as a burnt offering on one of the mountains, which I will show you." The next morning Abraham got up early. He saddled his donkey and took two of his servants with him, along with his son, Isaac. Then he chopped wood for a fire for a burnt offering and set out for the place God had told him about. On the

third day of their journey, Abraham looked up and saw the place in the distance. "Stay here with the donkey," Abraham told the servants. "The boy and I will travel a little farther. We will worship there, and then we will come right back."

So Abraham placed the wood for the burnt offering on Isaac's shoulders, while he himself carried the fire and the knife. As the two of them walked on together, Isaac turned to Abraham and said, "Father?" "Yes, my son?" Abraham replied. "We have the fire and the wood," the boy said, "but where is the sheep for the burnt offering?" "God will provide a sheep for the burnt offering, my son," Abraham answered. And they both walked on together.

When they arrived at the place where God had told him to go, Abraham built an altar and arranged the wood on it. Then he tied his son, Isaac, and laid him on the altar on top of the wood. And Abraham picked up the knife to kill his son as a sacrifice. At that moment, the angel of the Lord called to him from heaven, "Abraham! Abraham!" "Yes," Abraham replied. "Here I am!"

"Don't lay a hand on the boy!" the angel said. "Do not hurt him in any way, for now I know that you truly fear God. You have not withheld from me even your son, your only son."

Then Abraham looked up and saw a ram caught by its horns in a thicket. So he took the ram and sacrificed it as a burnt offering in place of his son. Abraham named the place Yahweh-Yireh (which means, "The Lord will provide"). To this day, people still use that name as a proverb: "On the mountain of the Lord it will be provided."

Then the angel of the Lord called again to Abraham from heaven. "This is what the Lord says: Because you have obeyed me and have not withheld even your son, your only son, I swear by my own name that I will certainly bless you. I will multiply your descendants beyond number, like the stars in the sky and the sand on the seashore. Your descendants will conquer the cities of their enemies. And through your descendants all the nations of the earth will be blessed — all because you have obeyed me."

Then they returned to the servants and travelled back to Beersheba, where Abraham continued to live.

Jerusalem was built on the Mountain of the Lord and became the city of God. It started as an altar built for sacrifice - a picture of the work of Jesus on the cross. Abraham is the key human character in this first incident involving the "seed bed" of Jerusalem and he shows the character of those who dwell in her.

- 22:2 "Here am I" – (they are listeners to and hearers of God)
- 22:2 "Take your son, whom you love very much and go" (they are tested and pioneers)
- 22:2 They have an individual response
- 22:2 They are people of sacrifice
- 22:3 Obedient to God
- 22:14 They are mountain seekers
- 22:9 Built from stone (individual character and variety)
- 22:9 Humble (laid all on the altar)
- 22:12 Live in freedom (result of obedience)
- 22:14 Clarity

We will consider these qualities in more depth shortly.

Abraham was a descendant of Shem (Gen11:10-26). The writer of the book of Hebrews testifies that Abraham was a man who was looking for a city with eternal foundations, designed and built by God (Heb 11:10). He did not receive that city, but had a vision for her, and welcomed her from a distance. (Heb 11:13). He had faith that he would be part of that city and God commended him for it. Let me now emphasise - we too can be part of that city, if we choose.

The rapid growth of Babylon compared to the slow growth of Israel is enlightening. Abraham was a man of faith in God and God counts it as righteousness to him (Romans 4:3). Nimrod, the founder of Babylon, was a man who depended on his own strength. Abraham was a friend of God. Nimrod did not follow Him. 'Babylon' grew rapidly and became a global centre - because she accepted anyone who wanted to find security in her. 'Jerusalem' grew slowly - because God only accepts people who have a relationship with Him. In Genesis 22, we find the foundations of Jerusalem. Having found a man who was willing to walk with Him and grow in faith and obedience, God looks for others to become a city.

Let us look at these people.

1.2 Listeners to and hearers of God

In Genesis 22:1, we read that God called Abraham. The transcript tells us that God just called his name. Not many words, but Abraham heard. He was listening. Do we hear God? Surely, it is a basic requirement for a God - follower. Probably the most common request I hear is to tell someone what God is saying to them. Why is this? The reason is that people do not have a relationship with God. Churches teach them to listen to a preacher, or to come to a decision through reasoning. They do not generally teach them how to listen to the Holy Spirit.

Abraham is a picture of all who dwell in spiritual "Jerusalem". He made many mistakes; very few of the decisions in his early life recorded in the bible are good decisions. Nonetheless, he had a relationship with God. He had faith in God. We know from Paul that faith comes from hearing the word of God (Rom 10:17).

Hearing depends on having something to hear - and that is where our relationship with God starts. It is no good if someone else tells us what God is saying unless we can be certain that it is God speaking through that person. Our faith has to be in God, not the person speaking. If our faith is not in God then it is in the person and we are putting him or her as our god.

God called Abraham and asked him to leave his country, relatives and home and go to a new land (Gen 12:1). His father, Terah, had started on this journey but stopped at the halfway point so God called Abraham to continue by himself. It is the same for us. If we stop where our parents have chosen to settle we will not fulfil our own purpose in God. Alternatively, children may stop whilst the parent continues with God. We are responsible for our own decisions.

Abraham listened to God. He was by himself; not part of a large group. Yes, he had a family, servants, and many people around him. But he was walking with God by himself. There may have been others walking with God as well - but it was their personal response to Him that was important, not a response as part of a group. This should be the same for us. We each have many relationships, but the relationship with God is the stimulus for all the others. Paul writes to God's people in Colosse and tells them the basic requirement to be in the Body of Christ is that we are connected to the Head, that is - Jesus (Col 1:18-23). We are individually different, with different gifts and purposes. But we can only be part of Christ's body if we are connected to Him.

I had a Christian couple come to me one day who asked if I thought they should be married. I asked them to tell me what God said about it. It is not my role - any person's role - to tell people what they should do unless God has clearly spoken. Even then, we should only advise. The decision has to be made by the one - or as in the case above, the couple - who will have to walk the journey. The couple, though, could not hear God, which is common enough when emotions are strong. I suggested, therefore, that they pray and fast for a few days in order to listen for an answer. They did so and both returned with words they felt were from God. When the tests came to the relationship over the next years, the couple were able to find peace in what God had told them.

There is an erroneous doctrine prevalent in the church about the Body of Christ. The doctrine says something like this: God loves His people and has made us His Body. Within the Body, there are leaders who have authority over people, responsible for bringing them to unity and maturity in Christ. The leaders know God better than other people. They are responsible for explaining Him and His requirements to His Body. In turn, the Body must submit to the leaders because God has given them responsibility for this.

The first statement that God loves His people and made us His Body is correct. The assumption following is incorrect. The whole emphasis of the New Testament is that we have an individual relationship with God; we are not part of His Body without this relationship. It is out of this relationship that we know who we are in God - our purpose, gifts and place in His Body. If I cannot hear God at all, I have to question my relationship with Him.

There will be times when a specific issue is not clear; but that is an exception rather than the rule, in contrast to the clarity over other issues.

The statement that there are leaders with responsibility to bring unity and maturity is incorrect. The Holy Spirit has that responsibility and authority, not people. He is in all the people of God. And the Holy Spirit uses whomever He wants, at different times, to fulfil His purposes. Eph 4:11-13 states that Jesus gave gifts to the Church. Verse 11 is usually mistranslated to put an emphasis on people and titles but in the original language, the words used are doing, active ones, not passive. A better translation becomes "He is the one who gives gifts to the Church to give messages, prophesy, evangelise, care for, and teach each other. The responsibility of these gifts is to equip God's people etc". It is Jesus who is the Good Shepherd, the Teacher, Apostle, Prophet, and Evangelist, and He fulfils these things through the Holy Spirit in His people.

If we choose to allow leaders to rule over us, we have departed to Babylon.

People argue that without leaders nothing gets done. They argue that leaders are required to head activities such as Church meetings. These arguments are only true for Babylonian meetings. They do not apply for the people of God who are able to respond to the Holy Spirit. Such Spirit-filled people do not need leaders but do require submissive spirits to each other. They do need to communicate together and be humble.

In "Babylon", Church meetings require leadership because people are not given freedom to listen to God: the programme followed requires certain things to take place. There is usually a programme of singing, praying, and a word, with an occasional prophecy - all allowed only under the control of someone who is in overall charge.

In a time when the people of God come together there should be no such restraint. There would normally be fewer people involved, perhaps from 2 to 20, and no-one would have a predetermined idea of what will – or "should"- take place. Individuals may have an idea of his or her own contribution if the Holy Spirit has prepared them, but not a 'programme' for the entire meeting. Sometimes there may be singing, sometimes not. There may be a prophecy or teaching, but it could be something else; it depends what the Holy Spirit is doing at the time.

This should be the norm for any time that God's people are together but an example may help to describe a "typical" meeting. I was with a group of 15 people - some mature and some immature Christians - who were meeting to spend time with each other and God. We had devoted two days to listen to the Holy Spirit together. During that time, the Holy Spirit was talking to us through many people and different gifts. We sang very little - perhaps two songs. On one of the days we started by someone reading a short passage from a book that God was using to speak to them. Someone else followed this by sharing a dream of the previous night. We spent some time seeking an interpretation of the dream. Someone else had a vision; another had a word of teaching. And so it went on. Each contribution did not have an immediate connection with the previous one.

Nonetheless, after 2 hours and a rich variety of contribution from everyone a clear understanding of what God was wanting became obvious. We needed the whole Body to be speaking in order to hear the whole Word.

Was there a leader? Yes, the Holy Spirit led through all who spoke. No human could have engineered the flow of life and word in the way that God did during that time together.

Times with God will always be different. He is a God of variety. But if we cannot hear Him how can we respond to Him? Abraham heard one word and immediately responded by saying "Here I am" (Gen 21:1). He was a listener and hearer of God.

1.3 They are tested and Pioneers

God tested Abraham on his faith and obedience. God asked him to go on a journey that would end in a request for him to sacrifice his son, Isaac. Abraham had waited many years for this promised son and now God was asking him to sacrifice the promise. I wonder if Abraham knew the importance of this request. Did he know that the place chosen by God for the sacrifice would become the city of Jerusalem? Did he know that God would request the sacrifice on the same mountain that Jesus would, many years later, also be sacrificed? I doubt it. It is only with our hindsight that we know that God would not require him to go through with the ordeal. With hindsight, we can see it as a picture of the future events concerning Jesus. Whatever Abraham knew, it was a singularly important journey on which he set out, in response to God. No one had been that way before. Abraham was a pioneer.

Pioneers inhabit Jerusalem; people who are prepared to go where God takes them in obedience to Him. Many people are pioneers, not only Christians. A pioneer is a person who leads the way into a new enterprise or adventure, such as a businessperson starting a new company or a researcher into new areas of science. Being a pioneer does not automatically give entrance into Jerusalem; there has to be the call of God as well.

God calls a pioneer to go on a journey, which is different for each person.

Like Abraham, God calls Christians - and they respond by going. The calling births a pioneering spirit and the response is to fulfil the reason for the calling. We read of Abraham's call in Genesis 11 - a call for a lifetime. In Genesis 22, we read of a call for a short-term test. On both occasions, he responded in obedience. When did God call you and for what purpose? There are many who attend Church who have not responded to a call; who do not realise their purpose.

When we hear a call from God, we find out why He created us. Paul informs us that many are called, but few are chosen. And many are called, but few respond - either because they do not hear or they decide the call is too hard. Jesus spoke a parable of a wealthy man who prepared a feast and called many guests to come but they all gave excuses and refused. If we want to dwell in Jerusalem, we need to respond to the call.

There is a palpable difference between those who hear their calling and those who do not. Those who have heard have a purpose and a destination to which they are moving. Paul could say at the end of his life, "*I have fought a good fight and run a good race. Now I am ready to receive the reward*" He knew his calling from the beginning (Acts 9:15). I know many people that God has called. They have a unique purpose - perhaps to write a book or to manage a business; to live with a foreign people and work out the kingdom of God. Each call is unique.

God called Abraham to go to a land, which God was going to give him, and to receive a son - the first of many. It sounds a simple calling. But it set in motion God's plan to redeem His people. It was the means God used to change Abraham's life; for him to become a God-fearer instead of an idol worshipper. It changed Abraham from being an indecisive, fearful person into one who could chase kings in battle; from being a disobedient doubter to an obedient man of faith; from a barren man to a fruitful father.

Not only did the calling change Abraham it also changed many of the people coming after him. He became the father of the faithful, which includes all who put their faith in Jesus.

God tested Abraham on his obedience and faith in the calling. Nothing is ever easy. Preachers will often give the impression that when we walk with God life is full of roses. This is not a true reflection of a Christian's life. The truth is that we go through many difficulties, allowed by God in order to train us and develop character, and often because of our poor decisions.

If we are to dwell in spiritual Jerusalem, we need faith in and obedience to Jesus. It is not enough to declare that we have faith and obedience; they have to be genuine. God tests us so that we know how genuine they are. Jesus spoke a parable of houses built on sand and houses built on rock (Matthew 7:24-27) to demonstrate that there is always testing to prove what is genuine.

James tells us that faith without works is dead (James 2:14-26) and cites the example of Abraham as a man of faith and obedience.

It is relatively easy to declare that you are a follower of Jesus, although this is becoming more difficult even in western society, which is rapidly becoming an antichrist environment. It is more difficult to live as a genuine follower of Jesus, because this involves a relationship with Him. Jesus is real and looks for reality in His people. He tests to see what reality has been formed in us. We, my wife and I, have experienced this on many occasions.

At the beginning of our marriage, and for a number of years afterwards, in common with most young newly weds, we rarely had enough money to cover the bills so we learnt to live by faith. And regularly we found a miraculous supply of food or money coming from surprising sources. One day we were running low on finance, with barely enough to cover until the next pay cheque in two weeks, when the Holy Spirit surprised us by asking us to give what we had to a visitor. A surprise and a struggle; but having struggled obedience won and the money was handed over. The visitor wrote a few days later to explain how the money had rescued him from a difficult situation, which explained to us why the Holy Spirit asked us to give. We also received in the post the following day some money to pay our own bills from an unexpected source. In His love, God was meeting the needs of His people and testing for reality.

We can only live in Jerusalem if we have reality. Jesus is reality. He said, "I am the way, the truth and the life" (John 14:6). The word "truth" in this verse means reality. Jesus was saying that He is true in every respect. Everything about Him is real. We become real through His work in us. Relationship with Jesus comes through calling and a faith response to Him. Obedience to calling forms a pioneering character within us. Testing proves the reality of this to us. Without testing, we do not know how deep the reality is and so, God tests each one of His people.

1.4 They have an individual response

When Abraham heard the call from God, his response is illuminating. He had reached old age and learnt much as he had walked with God through his life and his responses were now more considered. There are many responses he could have made to God's request for him to sacrifice Isaac. He could have run away, as Jonah did many years later when he did not want to obey a difficult request (Jonah 1 : 2&3). He could have argued, like Moses, that he was ill equipped for the task. But he does none of these: he packs his donkey, collects his son, and goes.

It was a very personal response. God was speaking to Abraham, and Abraham obeyed. He did not try to find the support of others. He did not take a large group with him; he just obeyed. Today, a Christian's response is often very different. Rather than immediate personal obedience, people will seek to impose their response on others expecting that everyone will respond to the word they have received, and go with them, failing to realise that God deals with us individually and at different times.

Several years ago, I spent some time in a particular organised Church. For 2 years, I felt God talking to me about the importance of relationships with His people. I talked about this with others during this time with no great response and after two years the Holy Spirit started to talk to me about a new issue and I stopped talking about relationships. However, almost immediately, after I stopped talking about relationships, the leadership of that group started to talk about them, putting pressure on people in this respect. As this issue was no longer what the Holy Spirit was asking me to talk about, I became involved with what He was talking about instead. The lesson I learnt from the experience was that God deals with us individually and at different times. Perhaps the two years I had been speaking about relationships were necessary for others as well as me - but they were mainly important for me - as that was what God was doing with me at the time.

Abraham had learnt that lesson as well. God was not asking everyone to sacrifice their sons; it was an individual request to Abraham, and he obeyed individually.

Abraham was prepared to be different from others. He had been different for many years living as an alien in the middle of the tribes of the land - tribes with different customs and gods. These tribes were involved with child sacrifice – not a custom Abraham followed. Unlike the tribes around him, he had no land of his own. He did not purchase any until his wife Sarah died and he needed a burial plot (Genesis 23). He was a stranger to these tribes and practices. He followed a different God.

When God asked him to sacrifice Isaac, Abraham obeyed, believing for resurrection. He did not respond in hopelessness as the tribes around him when they sacrificed their children. He obeyed believing that God would restore Isaac to him. He obeyed knowing that Isaac was the son through whom he would become a mighty nation, as God had promised.He obeyed knowing that God's word to him would be fulfilled; he had God's word on the subject, and he believed.

There are times when God speaks to a larger number of people together - the day of Pentecost is an example of this (Acts 2). On this day, the Holy Spirit came to earth and all present in the upper room were impacted by Him and caught up in the experience. But even on this day there was an individual response. Each person spoke with a new tongue, different for each person, but it was only Peter who stood up to speak to the crowds. Peter had previously been told by Jesus that he was being given the keys to open the kingdom (Matthew 16:19) so he was the only one who could stand up and speak.

Our response to God has to be on the foundation of His promises to us as individuals. That is why we have to respond personally: no one else has received those words God has given us - they were only for us.

When we initially respond to God, putting our trust in Him for the life that will follow, we become part of the Body of Christ. As part of this Body, we will work out our decisions and responses in partnership with many people but this is not what I am talking about when considering Abraham and his response when God calls him to sacrifice. I will consider our relationships with others in the Body of Christ later as we look at Jerusalem.

1.5 They are people of sacrifice

The words of Jesus in Matthew 16:24 are quite clear *"If anyone would come after me they must deny themselves and take up their cross and follow me"*. Someone taking up their cross was going to one place only - death. The popular message of today is that God will bless you. Contrast this with the message of Jesus that we are to deny ourselves and go to death.

It is true that God blesses us. We are the inheritors of amazing blessings. God heals, provides, gives life in abundance, and finds many ways to bless us each day. Nonetheless, this was not the main emphasis of the message of Jesus. He was more concerned with us seeking Him and His Kingdom; seeking the death of our natural desires and strength. The "God will bless you" message tends to encourage selfishness and soul growth rather than spiritual growth. By soul growth, I mean the ability of man to do things by himself without the involvement of the Spirit of God. This is in opposition to the work of God in us performed by the Holy Spirit.

The people of God are people of sacrifice. We receive our new life through the sacrifice of Jesus. We find that life through death to our reliance on natural abilities and desires. Unless we die to these things we cannot really live or produce real fruit. The process of fruitfulness is through death because unless a seed falls into the earth and dies it will not produce fruit.

The message from God that He wants to bless is often misunderstood. The words "God will bless" are often spoken to the sick, the poor, or those hurting in other ways. They imply that God will rescue the person concerned from the difficulty, the sickness, the hard situation, and make all things different. The truth is that God is more interested in the long-term development of a person's spiritual life than in the short term easing of pain. If a sickness will draw a person to Him, the sickness becomes a blessing. If a bankruptcy draws a person to spiritual life, it becomes a blessing - far more than the supply of money to pay a debt. God wants us to reach a place of sacrifice. It is better to lose health if it means the receiving of the kingdom of God.

Jesus told us that His kingdom is within us. Most people look for an external kingdom, one that makes them look and feel good. Daniel teaches that the kingdom of God will eventually knock down every other kingdom and people look for an external evidence of this - expecting the kingdoms of the world to fall. That will eventually happen when Jesus returns. But for us, today, the kingdom is within. It is a kingdom of power to change us, and through us the world. It is a kingdom that grows through the individual response of people and through spiritual warfare - not through human wars.

The power of the kingdom of God is released through the sacrifice of her people. If we die to self- government and the reliance on self-ability, we become the medium through whom the Holy Spirit can work. If we do not die in this way, we remain full of self-ability only. Death to self-government deals with our natural ability to withstand God. Natural man opposes God. We always have done since the time of Adam. Natural man has considerable ability and can do much that looks good. We saw earlier that the builders of the Tower of Babel had much ability. They could have achieved much had God not brought them confusion. Natural man can persuade others to live "better" lives through New Year resolutions, meditation, and other self-help techniques. But this is not the same as death to reliance on the self-life. Natural man's power is used instead of God or, in biblical terms, anti-Christ.

Death to self-reliance is the result of a decision to give the Holy Spirit freedom in our life; to obey Him rather than rely on our own ability. As the prophet, Zechariah, said, *"It is not by might nor by power but by my Spirit"* (Zech 4:6). Death comes through the work of the Holy Spirit. Paul writes that the sinful nature of man is cut off through baptism (Col 2:11). We are buried with Christ when we are baptised and we are then raised to a new life in the Holy Spirit. There is a sacrifice of our sinful nature at the beginning our life with Christ.

Many Christians go through baptism and have their sinful nature cut away, only to continue life afterwards as if nothing had happened. They go on living from their natural resources instead of the Holy Spirit. Without a revelation of what God is doing in baptism, there is no visible benefit in going through the motions of baptism.

Baptism is the initial opportunity to die to self. It is the initial opportunity to pick up our cross. We carry the cross for life: it is no longer the self, "I", that should live but Christ living through us. Are we more interested in our comfort and ease than the life of Christ within us?

God asked Abraham to put everything on the altar. His dreams, his son, his whole purpose, the promises - everything was being sacrificed. He had nothing left except the God who was asking him to make the sacrifice. The blessing of God was to come through sacrifice. Abraham did not know that. But he believed.

The kingdom of God is within us and grows through sacrifice. Our usefulness to God depends on how much we let Him rule in our lives at the cost to self-rule. The less we depend on self-ability and the more we depend on the Holy Spirit, the more God will release His power and resources to us.

How much are we prepared to trust God? There is a simple, but difficult answer. God wants us to trust Him totally. Not in part. Totally. Complete trust, regardless of the consequences. He does not promise us a life of ease and prosperity but one of conflict and difficulty with Him. In John 16:33 we read, *"I have told you all this so that you may have peace in me. Here on earth you will have many trials and sorrows. But take heart, because I have overcome the world."* If He were not in this life, it would be beyond bearing - but with Him comes His promise to stay with us. And because we have that promise we can experience His presence, His peace, and His Spirit with us through all circumstances.

God's rescue plans are well known. They usually arrive at the last minute or even, seemingly, too late as Lazarus found out (John 11). How many Christians have believed for healing only to die, or for finance only to find bankruptcy? Did God fail? Of course, not: His plans are for our internal, kingdom growth-not just our external comfort. Often, as we go through the tough situations God is looking for sacrifice rather than rescue. Unless we die to self, we cannot really live.

1.6 They are obedient to God

Obedience to God should be straightforward. Yet it rarely is. The problem is in our hardness of heart, our deafness. If God spoke with an audible voice, if we heard clearly and loudly, our response would be much easier. But He rarely does speak in this way. Instead, He chooses the soft whisper of the wind. He waits for our responses; for us to pick up His vibrations. Even Paul writing to the Corinthians resorts to what he believes God would say rather than what he knows God has said (1 Cor 7:25-28). He says, "*Now regarding your question about the young women who are not yet married. I do not have a command from the Lord for them. But the Lord in his mercy has given me wisdom that can be trusted, and I will share it with you. Because of the present crisis, I think it is best to remain as you are. If you have a wife, do not seek to end the marriage. If you do not have a wife, do not seek to get married. But if you do get married, it is not a sin. And if a young woman gets married, it is not a sin. However, those who get married at this time will have troubles, and I am trying to spare you those problems.*" Reading this passage today we have to ask whether the words are still relevant Paul was talking about the pressures of that century, when the Romans were killing all Christians and Paul wanted to protect them.

Theoretically, the more mature we are in our walk with God, the easier it is to hear and understand Him. Even so, this is not always the case. We will have times in the "wilderness" when it seems that God has deserted us, when the heavens seem closed. New Christians usually have times of clarity in hearing God. The Holy Spirit seems to take delight in communicating with people who are new to a relationship with Him. For more mature

Christians the Holy Spirit takes a different delight, in their growth and training.

It is vital that we learn to hear God and understand Him before seeking to be obedient to Him. If we do not we can be doing, and saying, things which have no meaning. As a younger Christian, I have been in groups where a person might feel "God" saying things such as "we should stand on chairs" with no obvious retrospective purpose. People who did not hear God but only their imaginations have sent me on many wild goose chases.

Sometimes we hear God through others, as did Paul and Barnabas. They were enjoying a time with other people who taught and prophesied when the Holy Spirit spoke to them about travelling to other places (Acts 13:1-3). *"Among the prophets and teachers of the church at Antioch of Syria were Barnabas, Simeon (called "the black man"), Lucius (from Cyrene), Manaen (the childhood companion of King Herod Antipas), and Saul. One day as these men were worshiping the Lord and fasting, the Holy Spirit said, "Dedicate Barnabas and Saul for the special work to which I have called them." So after more fasting and prayer, the men laid their hands on them and sent them on their way."*

Sometimes we talk to others when we are confused, finding clarity through the conversation. The important thing is eventually to hear God's voice. We do so by looking for the Holy Spirit in the people we speak to, and the things we read - for He lives in each one of God's people. I have a friend who is going through a period when he cannot watch a film without hearing God speak to Him as He is looking for God wherever he is. The danger is that when we listen to others we hear their opinions, instead of God's voice; we need to be able to distinguish between them. In fact, it is imperative that we do lest we become obedient to people rather than God.

Obedience to God is a fundamental characteristic of someone wanting to walk with God. If we do not obey Him, we are in rebellion against Him. It is not valid to argue that you obeyed another person if that obedience took you into an action that God did not require. There is an account of such an incident reported in 1 Kings 13. A prophet from Judah went to Bethel and denounced King Jereboam at the instruction of God. God specifically told him that he must not return the same way as he went and must not eat food nor drink water until he had returned to Judah (v9). A different, old, prophet living in Bethel decided to tempt the younger man (we are not told why) and overtook him on his return journey. The old prophet said that an angel had sent him to take the younger man to his home to provide food and water, so persuading the younger prophet to disobey the Lord. Whilst they were eating, the Lord gave the old prophet a real word of rebuke for the younger man; the young prophet would die because of his disobedience. There was no room for him to argue that he was obeying a man of God, even though the old prophet was clearly recognised as such.

Many people set themselves up as God's spokesperson, and they may be just that. But no one is always accurate in what they say all the time; usually they are only partly accurate at the best of times. I have received many words from people and found them very helpful generally. Nonetheless, I have had to test every word, as to the spirit from which it comes, and understand each particular word by the Spirit. (All prophetic words need to be tested whether given to an individual or a group.) I received some words from people living with a Church perspective but could only work them out from a Kingdom revelation. Sometimes people give words when they have an axe to grind and the words have to be unwrapped carefully, or simply discarded. The responsibility for our life is ours and we cannot hand it to someone else. We cannot blame others for the mistakes we make.

When God speaks, we need to obey. But the timing has to be right. Sometimes God gives a long warning of what He wants; at other times none at all. To obey at the wrong time can be as bad as disobedience. God wants us to learn to hear Him clearly and walk in step with Him. (Gal 5:25)

The central verses in the bible are Psalm 118:8 - 9. These say, "*It is better to take refuge in the Lord than to trust in people. It is better to take refuge in the Lord than to trust in princes.*" Obedience is difficult, if not impossible, without trust. God asks us to trust Him rather than man.

1.7 They are Mountain seekers

Physical Jerusalem, built on a series of mountains, is a mixture of old and new. The site of much of biblical Jerusalem is mainly an archeological site or been rebuilt since the destruction in AD70. Visitors to the city on foot find themselves on a mountainside with some serious slopes. The site of the Temple is on one of the smaller mountains and Abraham is likely to have travelled to this point to make his sacrifice. Without the use of cars or roads and through tough terrain, it must have been an arduous journey. Nevertheless, he made the journey willingly, in anticipation of finding God there.

Just as physical Jerusalem is built on the mountains, spiritual Jerusalem is found in the spiritual mountains. Jesus said that it is those who seek Him who find Him and He gave several illustrations of what He meant by seeking. In Matthew 7:7, we read, "*Keep on asking, and you will receive what you ask for. Keep on seeking, and you will find. Keep on knocking, and the door will be opened to you.*" In Luke 15, we find three parables that talk of the determination of God in seeking us, rather than showing how we should seek Him. Nevertheless, they do show the persistence we need in our search. The first parable is about the shepherd who leaves everything and everyone in order to search for a lost sheep. He searches the mountains through difficult and impossible terrain until he finds what he is looking for. The second parable concerns a woman who has lost a coin; she searches through the dirt and forgotten places until she finds it. The third parable concerns the Father who is full of love and compassion and waits constantly on the alert looking in faith every day for his rebellious son to return to him. Searching involves persistence, patience, application, and faith.

We need to climb the mountains to live with God. They speak of an obstacle that we must overcome. Some are small and some huge - but they all have to be overcome in order to enjoy the experience found at the summit.The view from the heights of a mountain is different to that in the valleys. In the valley, everything is near; the buildings and landscape around cut off distance. On the summit, the view is far and panoramic, with nothing to stop the eye from seeing all that is around. It is a place where we can see perspective. A place where those things that looked impossibly large when we were in the valley look minute from the perspective on the mountain.

It takes application to climb the mountain, and many are not motivated for the effort; never experience the mountaintop. The age in which we live does not encourage people to be patient and apply energy to obtaining a goal. We live in a throwaway society; easy come, easy go - in a society that expects to be able to push a button and have instant gratification, whether for food or relaxation. Credit is easy. No need to wait until the money is real before buying something outright when we can have it now and pay later. Modern society does not embrace the skills needed for seeking God. People do not know how to wait patiently for Him to come. Even in places where God's people meet together, where we come with the intent to honour God, there is rarely time spent waiting on Him. Instead, there is instant gratification through bands, choirs, and prepared words in order to keep things moving so that the audience is not bored. The Kingdom of God is not a place where we should expect instant gratification in this way.

God's ways are different from those of man. He waits for us to come into line with Him. When we meet together, it should be to hear Him and not ourselves. We need to quieten our spirits, quieten our minds, in order to hear Him before speaking and becoming involved in action. Much of what is offered to God under the guise of worship is just hot air and empty words: it comes from soulish emotion and is not a response of spirit to Spirit.

Abraham travelled a long way before he reached his destination; the place of worship. It took time and application before he was ready and in God's time and place. But when the right time and place had been reached God stepped into Abraham's world. He heard the voice of God giving direction and renewing the promises. If we are more patient and spend time seeking Him, we also will experience God.

1.8 Built from stone

We see in our story of Abraham and the sacrifice of Isaac that there is a need for an altar. God required that Abraham built this from stone. We considered that God uses stone rather than brick when looking at Babylon's roots. The characteristics of stone differ from that of bricks in many significant ways, and God uses these building blocks to show the importance of these characteristics in His people.

One of the properties of stones is that the Master Builder can create unique shapes through chipping. Bricklayers do cut bricks - into halves, or thirds etc - but they cannot shape them in the same way as stone; bricks are intrinsically brittle. How brittle are we? Do we collapse when circumstances are difficult? Or do we have staying power to allow the circumstances to mould us into a unique shape?

Few people take their problems first to God before going to the secular places of "wisdom". If we have a cold, the first place to go is the doctor's surgery. If we need money, the bank will give a loan. Whatever the problem, there is a secular answer that offers instant solutions rather than the patient waiting on the Lord. God allows many problems in our lives in order to mould us into a unique shape. We create a different shape from His desired option by finding our secular answers.

Abraham knew what it was like for God to shape his life and character. He began life living in a land where people worshipped lifeless gods and sacrificed their children to them. The God of life called him to leave the place and gods of his childhood and go to a land that God would give him and his heirs if they worshipped Him as the only true God. Abraham left his origins and in doing so placed himself into the hands of the Master craftsman who began His work of remoulding Abraham's character. He encountered many setbacks and difficulties through which he eventually learnt to trust God. The process was not easy, nor without many failures. When we read the life of Abraham, it is to see a loving and forgiving God embracing a failed man. Through his failure, Abraham learnt many lessons; he became a man whom God called "friend". He also became the man from whom God was pleased to produce his children of promise, firstly as the nation Israel and later as all His people who walk with Him through the accomplishment of Jesus.

Abraham did not find the moulding process easy. Often he made decisions that on the face of it could make his life easier; in reality, those decisions caused severe difficulties. He often took matters into his own hands rather than waiting for God, as in the situation of having an heir. For example, God promised him a son but after many years, the fulfilment of the promise did not seem likely. He was old, at a time in life when he was getting past natural productivity. In short, he must have felt that time was running out. So he decided to have a child through his servant girl instead of his wife. This he managed, proving that infertility was not his problem. But the child that was born became a thorn in his flesh, in Sarah's flesh - and in the flesh of all who survive today. In his anxiety and desperation, Abraham failed to trust God. He trusted his own ability - only to reap devastation. It is through this and many other difficulties that we see Abraham changing until he is ready for the test of the sacrifice of his son. We can look at Abraham with hindsight and see that he became a man of faith - but the formation of this in him took a lifetime.

Jacob is a good example of a man who turned his back on God's solutions in order to find his own answers and give himself a "good life". Genesis chapters 25 to 49 tell the story. He was a liar, a swindler, a thief and had many other undesirable traits until God met with him as he ran away from his father- in-law, Laban. He had spent his life up to this point avoiding the pressure of the Master Builder, doing all he could to make his life easy. But his plans were rapidly unwinding: he had Laban chasing him from behind and an irate brother, Esau, coming towards him whose last stated intent was to kill him. God chose this time to make His move. He waited until Jacob had sent his wives, children, servants and cattle away before stepping into the arena with him. Jacob had no idea that his difficult situation would become worse as he faced the angel of God unless he was prepared to submit to Him.

Jacob wrestled with God. He was still a hard, brittle person with no intention of changing. But God desired otherwise. At the end of the night, He touched the hip of Jacob, and from that moment onwards, Jacob limped; he would never be the same again. In fact, God changed his name to Israel, to show that he was now a different person. He needed the aid of a stick to walk around. His character and lifestyle became different and we see how he started to hate the old ways that had previously held him prisoner. If he had remained a brick-like character, none of this would have been possible: the process would have shattered him.

The altar, the place of worship and sacrifice, was made of stone. People who wish to be similarly involved with worship and sacrifice need to have the same characteristics. We must be people who allow God to change us: people who know that He allows many circumstances to enter our lives to mould us. This involves trust. Trust in His love and handiwork coupled with a desire for Him to work His character into us.

1.9 Humble

Humility does not come easily to anyone. But it has to come if we are to walk with God. Abraham did not start as a humble man. He needed some moulding before he could accept that God's ways are best. He spent much of his life living with pride, as can be seen by the way he made his decisions independent of God. Pride encourages us to be independent of God and to live by self-government. Humility allows us to recognise what we really are and to bend to the will of God.

In 1Peter 5:5, we read that, "*God opposes the proud but favours the humble*". God is against the proud person but welcomes the humble. Spiritual Jerusalem is not a place for the self-seeker, the boaster, or person who pushes himself or herself forward for attention. Instead, we find those who are prepared to be nothing, if that is what is required; those who look for others to shine, if that is where the Holy Spirit can be found. A humble person knows his or her value and does not need to be valued higher through self - effort. Humility is not subservience but a proper appreciation of who you are in Christ. (Rom 12:3) If we are humble, we are able to take a lead when it is our responsibility but, equally able, without grudge, to pass that lead on to others when they are more useful in the role.

Abraham learnt humility eventually. God does not tell us how long Abraham lived in the city of Ur or how long he stayed with his father before he died. He informs us that he did not fully obey God until his natural parents had gone. Pride causes disobedience because we think we know better than God knows, or are unwilling to trust Him. Humility recognises that God is greater than man and can be obeyed and trusted at all times.

Abraham went through several situations in his earlier life when he did not trust God, which gives the impression that he was not then humble. He ran to Egypt when there was a drought and lived there for a time (Gen 12:10 onwards). God did not tell him to go but it seems he thought it a good idea to go. While there, he relied on duplicity to protect Sarah, but failed. As already mentioned he later tired of waiting for God to give him an heir and took matters into his own hands by having a son through his servant Hagar (Gen 16). Still later, he again trusted in his own plans when he went to Gerar, the land of Abimelech (Gen 20). Abimelech decided to take Sarah as a wife - she was a beautiful woman and Abraham had passed her off as his sister. Abraham may have thought he would reduce the likelihood of problems by doing this. Instead, he created more. Once again, though, God rescued him.

Even though he found it difficult to trust God, Abraham was changing through these difficulties until there comes the testing over the sacrifice of Isaac. At this point, Abraham seems to trust God absolutely, expecting for the resurrection of Isaac. It is from this time that Abraham became the model for the people of God. He had become humble.

1.10 Live in Freedom

In Galatians 5:1, Paul tells us, *"it was for freedom that we have been made free"*. He warns us not to return to bondage. I wonder if we understand what it is to be free.

Someone living with the pains of ill health yearns for freedom from pain and, if it comes, knows what freedom from pain means. The pain is a restriction that stops movement. It is a barrier to a certain amount of freedom. But this is only a small part of what Paul meant. The freedom he was talking about embraced everything that keeps a person bound. He meant freedom from the law and the effects of sin. Elsewhere he says, *"Everything is permissible, but not everything is sensible"*. Everything is permissible. But the law says that many things are not permissible. Sin, which becomes obvious by the law, is the reason that many things are not permissible. But, Jesus has fulfilled the requirements of the law; Jesus has overcome the effects of sin.

Many Christians still live under the law and the effects of sin, even though Jesus died and rose again to give them freedom. The law brings guilt and condemnation, stifling the freedom that Jesus gained. Freedom comes by living in submission to the will of Jesus and putting trust in Him.

Abraham obeyed God. He submitted to the will of God. And in doing so, he received freedom. In the incident that we are considering with Abraham (Genesis 22:12) the freedom he receives is from the requirement to sacrifice Isaac, but the principle is carried on into all aspects of life. He trusted God to do what He promised.

The Jerusalem that Christians desire to live in is a place of freedom inhabited by free people. It is freedom from sin and the effect of sin; freedom from fear and the power of fear. Can we live in this city today or do we have wait until it comes down from heaven at a later day?

Jesus told his disciples that the kingdom of heaven was at hand. He opened the door to this kingdom when He broke the kingdom of darkness through the victory of the cross. From that day onwards, the kingdom of heaven has been available to us. Yet, we are reticent to enter this kingdom and even more reticent to explore the depths that are not immediately obvious. It is as if some hidden chain holds us back from enjoying the delights of the kingdom of God.

Yet, Jesus bought our freedom. Abraham found freedom through obedience to God. We also find freedom through obedience to God.

People of freedom inhabit the Jerusalem we are considering. Today, we do not enjoy this city. Instead of freedom, the people of God continue to live in bondage. Sin is not defeated nor the effects of sin. The people of God continue to argue; fight; live in fear; accept the restrictions of the kingdom of darkness. Not so Abraham: He walked with God and learnt obedience.

1.11 Clarity

We saw that a characteristic of Babylon is confusion. The opposite is true of Jerusalem. God is light, bringing us into light, as we trust Him. Paul, writing to the Corinthians, says, *"We have the mind of Christ."* (1 Cor

2:16) Again, writing to the Corinthians, Paul says, *"Has Christ been divided into factions?"* (1 Cor 1:13) Many passages in the bible talk of the unity that comes from walking with God. When we consider the lack of unity and confusion of doctrine in the Church, it is obvious that we do not live as citizens of the New Jerusalem yet.

2.0 Adam

God has introduced us to many people in the bible. These people tell us much about Babylon and Jerusalem. We can see good character and bad. As we study them, we can understand something of God's intent.

Eternity is in the heart of man. From the beginning, God created man with a heart for eternity and with the permanence of eternity within. The first man, Adam, is usually remembered for introducing sin into the world. But there are other aspects of his life that are more relevant to our study. He enjoyed fellowship with God, perhaps for many years, before he sinned. He walked with God and communed with Him in the evenings. If we learn nothing else from Adam, we need to learn that

God wants fellowship with us. We major on his sin; but before the sin, it was fellowship, and after the sin God restored that fellowship, through sacrifice, and Adam continued to enjoy time with God. Adam is a good illustration of the type of people who live in the New Jerusalem; he knew how to fellowship with God.

Jerusalem is the place of fellowship. In OT times, Jerusalem was the site for the Temple, the place where the people found God waiting for them. In the New Jerusalem, there is no further need for a temple because God lives with His people. There is restored fellowship, lost by Adam, but regained by Jesus and taken to a new degree. Adam fellowshipped in the evening; we have fellowship all the time. God dwells with His people instead of just visiting at the cool of the day.

Fellowship is often misunderstood or understood with a shallow experience or intention. Many think of fellowship as a formal church meeting as seen in the term, "I'm off to the fellowship". This is only partially true. The act of going to a meeting does not automatically ensure fellowship with God. It may give fellowship with people, but often falls short of fellowship with God. This occurs when our spirit touches His Spirit and there is a transaction of life. This can take place as we meet with people, but the men and women of the bible often experienced this fellowship as they spent time with God alone. Adam and Eve walked with God together and fellowshipped with Him before sin contaminated relationships. They probably did so after God restored the relationship with Him, although we only read of the occasion when God pronounced the curses resulting from sin. They found an intimacy in their fellowship with God often missing from large groups.

The New Jerusalem will be a place of fellowship. Can we enjoy this fellowship with others today? The answer is "Yes." But we must first experience it with God before attempting to do so with others. Unless God takes us through the barriers to fellowship, we will find it difficult, if not impossible, to fellowship at any depth with people. Intimacy comes after God heals pain and hurts.

God also gave Adam the responsibility to rule over all created things. He gave this mandate before Adam sinned, and the responsibility was not onerous at that time. Without sin, there were no consequences. Adam did not have to sweat as he did later. Animals were not wild; weeds did not overcome the crops; he had nothing that was in rebellion to God. There was no self-interest, greed, lust, and the various corruptions of God's character. Adam only knew how to love and he ruled, for however long before he sinned, in love. Perhaps, God gave Adam this responsibility in order to bring Satan to heel. If Adam had heeded God's mandate, he would have realised that Satan was an enemy that needed to be ruled, but he did not. In the New Jerusalem, God again gives man the mandate to rule in love.

Ruling meant something different to Adam from what we understand today. We think of despots, torture, control, laws, submission, police, and many other things. To rule is to bring all things into line with the intentions of the ruler. In contrast, Adam thought only of the love of God and ensuring that everything was in line with His will and pattern. A rule is normally a straight line and a ruler ensures all things are in line. God gave Adam an instruction to rule, to bring all things in line with His intentions and plan and with His character.

God did not give Adam a mandate to rule over his fellow man. God retained this responsibility for Himself. In the corrupted world where man seeks to build his empires, man takes rulership; he corrupts it to become a tool to control others by whatever means is at hand. Whenever control is used to rule man, we see the character of Babylon, not Jerusalem.

When we listen to Jesus, however, we hear Him say through the writer of the book of Hebrews at 2:11-12, *"So now Jesus and the ones he makes holy have the same Father. That is why Jesus is not ashamed to call them his brothers and sisters. For he said to God, "I will proclaim your name to my brothers and sisters. I will praise you among your assembled people."* In exercising His right to rule, Jesus, instead of rising above others, lowers Himself to be an equal brother to His brothers and sisters. He becomes the firstborn among many brethren. He is born first but among many equals. Our response, surely, is to say, "This cannot be allowed" and to submit to His love and wisdom, putting Him at a higher place. But, as we understand the ways of His kingdom, we will find that He does not seek a higher place in rulership but an equal place in co-rulership. From our perspective, Jesus is the name above all others. And we find in Revelation (11.16) 24 elders falling on their faces before God (again in Rev19:4). We seek to submit to Him at all times and to worship Him. Paul teaches that we should submit to each other in Ephesians 5 and we find Jesus living to the same principle.

The character of Jerusalem that we find in Adam is twofold: fellowship with God, and ruling over creation in love. We see these characteristics in Jesus as well. He rose early in the morning to fellowship with His Father, sometimes spending the nights alone with Him. Creation obeyed Him to the amazement of those who saw the waves and storm becoming still; who saw an unbroken animal carrying Him on its back, and who saw the many other deeds of loving rule. In the New Jerusalem, we can expect these characteristics to grow in us.

A further aspect of the life of Adam is that he was an explorer. He had a new and unknown land in which he lived, with new creatures. He named the animals and explored the land, firstly, with God, and then, after he was expelled from the garden, as a way of life. Exploration, like pioneering, comes as we accept the challenges of life and seek ways of overcoming them. We considered the character of the pioneer as we looked at Babylon and I do not want to repeat what I said then. Suffice to say that we will have much to explore in the New Jerusalem, not only on this planet but also on the vast array of creation in skies.

3.0 Enoch

We do not know much about Enoch except that he walked with God throughout his life. He was an early descendant of Adam and Genesis 5 gives the ancestry table. Verse 18 tells us, *"When Jared was 162 years old, he became the father of Enoch. After the birth of Enoch,*

Jared lived another 800 years, and he had other sons and daughters. Jared lived 962 years, and then he died. When Enoch was 65 years old, he became the father of Methuselah. After the birth of Methuselah, Enoch lived in close fellowship with God for another 300 years, and he had other sons and daughters. Enoch lived 365 years, walking in close fellowship with God. Then one day he disappeared, because God took him."
His end was sudden and dramatic. Hebrews 11:5, tells us, *"It was by faith that Enoch was taken up to heaven without dying — "he disappeared, because God took him." For, before he was taken up, he was known as a person who pleased God."* He was a true son of Jerusalem.

Few people have left this world without dying. The bible recounts the lives of two people who managed this: Enoch and Elijah. It is possible that Moses was also part of this exclusive company, but there are contradictory accounts of his end. Even Jesus had to go through death, although for different reasons. The lesson from Enoch is that there is life after this world. He entered the new life without dying but all citizens of New Jerusalem will enjoy the life that he has found.

Enoch walked with God in intimacy. God enjoyed this so much He took Enoch with Him to continue that fellowship. Enoch seems to have lived a normal life. He was not a hermit; he married and had children. The distinction between him and others was that he enjoyed God far more. As a result, he entered his final reward early. It is not necessarily the evil who die young. Indeed, we are often left to wonder why those who clearly love God die early. But Enoch shows us that God loves intimacy with us and longs to continue that in Heaven.

4.0 Noah

Most Christians have heard about Noah (Genesis chapters 6-8). He is a man we learn about from an early age. We frequently use his life story to warn of God's judgement and explain God's salvation. Noah, like Enoch before, walked with God. But, he had a different destiny. Noah had a responsibility to build an ark and warn his generation of coming judgement.

We read that Noah was building the ark for one hundred years. He had probably never experienced rain before and lived a distance from the sea so had little understanding of the reason for building an ark – particularly one with such dimensions. But, Noah was obedient, skilled, and patient.

Noah lived with a generation who did not fear God. As he built the ark, his generation mocked and ridiculed him. As he offered a safe place to avoid judgement, they ignored him. Noah proclaimed the warning of God in his day by word and deed. He persevered through many difficulties.

The ark speaks of a safe place – an alternative to judgement. Noah chose the safe place that God offered, but he had to build it first. In our generation, God also offers a safe place to avoid judgement. But, it is not yet completed. The ark today is the corporate people of God.

Noah teaches us that the people of God are obedient and persevere, even though what God says does not immediately happen. He teaches us that the people of God need to be skilful in what they do. Without skill in working with wood, Noah could never have finished his task.

5.0 Moses

Moses had many characteristics. He was priest, lawgiver, leader, fighter, and father, amongst many others. But, above all else he was a friend of God.

Moses had a long life, often seen to be in three stages. As a child and up to early manhood, he was a product of Egypt. He used man's methods to obtain his goals, which included killing an Egyptian when he thought it justified – himself a Hebrew intervening on behalf of a Hebrew. At this stage we see Moses seeking to do God's will without His Spirit.

The second stage of the life of Moses was in the wilderness where he ran to escape the judgement of Pharoah. It is the place where God broke, and trained him; where He eventually called and commissioned him. God gave him individual training. He took him to a place where no one could meddle with God's purposes. It shows us how God chooses to relate with us. He takes us into wilderness places - not physical ones but spiritual. He moulds us by the work of His Spirit, not by the work of man's hands. It is not through training courses in the schools of man that we know God and His ways. It is as He walks with us through the hard times and we learn to trust Him and to depend on Him.

God walked with Moses for forty years in this wilderness until he was eighty years old. God knew how to forge his character and make a "stone" out of Egypt's "brick". When He knew he was ready, God told Moses that He had a purpose for him. He commissioned him to lead the Israelites out of captivity. Today, we need to learn how to let God train and develop us. We need to take our hands away unless we cause damage to what He does.

The third stage of the life of Moses was the last forty years as he showed the Israelites how to walk through the wilderness. He was then the leader of the nation. He was so because he walked closely with God. No one else walked close with God in the same way. Perhaps Joshua learnt how to do this as he served Moses but even he did not match Moses's life. The lesson for us to learn is that we cannot fulfil God's commission unless we walk closely with Him.

6.0 David

David was the king chosen by God to lead Israel after Saul. Saul was a king who relied on man's strength, and failed. David relied on God, and succeeded. In his youth, God called David a man after His own heart. Nonetheless, not everything David did was righteous. Not everything he did was sensible. But, he loved God and walked with Him.

However, much that David did was unhelpful. He built a Temple that God did not want. He developed Temple worship that has become a snare to much of Christendom today. He laid the foundation of hierarchy during his reign, which Solomon took to greater levels, to an extent that the heathen queen of Sheba was spellbound by what she saw.

Despite all this, God loved David. He was the king of Israel who is a picture of the coming King, Jesus. Like all the men and women of God, David's training was unique. He was a shepherd who learnt to listen to God whilst caring for the sheep on the mountains. He had battles with lions and bears. He sang songs accompanying himself with a harp. He was chased for many years by a madman, King Saul, who wanted to kill him. Through all these things, he learnt to trust God, and to be obedient.

David became the leader of a band of soldiers. At first, this was a band of thieves and scoundrels. David accepted them, as they accepted him. Perhaps this is one of the major parts of David's character. He accepted people, just as Jesus does today.

David was a servant, willing to do what was asked. He served his father by looking after the sheep. He served his brothers by delivering their food and supplies when on army duty. He served Saul by fighting Goliath and playing the harp to soothe his moods. He served the nation by being king. He served God as he obeyed throughout his life.

We too are called to be servants as well as kings. We cannot do the latter without being the former. Paul tells us that we reign with Christ and encourages us to see things from God's point of view – the view of reigning in the heavenlies. We cannot do this unless we are first of all servants. Jesus said, "He who wants to be the greatest must become the servant of all".

7.0 The Character of Jerusalem

In Revelation 21, John describes the New Jerusalem: *"Then I saw a new heaven and a new earth, for the old heaven and the old earth had disappeared. And the sea was also gone. And I saw the holy city, the new Jerusalem, coming down from God out of heaven like a bride beautifully dressed for her husband.*

I heard a loud shout from the throne, saying, "Look, God's home is now among his people! He will live with them, and they will be his people. God himself will be with them. He will wipe every tear from their eyes, and there will be no more death or sorrow or crying or pain. All these things are gone forever." And the one sitting on the throne said, "Look, I am making everything new!" And then he said to me, "Write this down, for what I tell you is trustworthy and true." And he also said, "It is finished! I am the Alpha and the Omega — the Beginning and the End. To all who are thirsty I will give freely from the springs of the water of life. All who are victorious will inherit all these blessings, and I will be their God, and they will be my children. "But cowards, unbelievers, the corrupt, murderers, the immoral, those who practice witchcraft, idol worshipers, and all liars — their fate is in the fiery lake of burning sulfur. This is the second death." Then one of the seven angels who held the seven bowls containing the seven last plagues came and said to me, "Come with me! I will show you the bride, the wife of the Lamb."

So he took me in the Spirit to a great, high mountain, and he showed me the holy city, Jerusalem, descending out of heaven from God. It shone with the glory of God and sparkled like a precious stone — like jasper as clear as crystal. The city wall was broad and high, with twelve gates guarded by twelve angels. And the names of the twelve tribes of Israel were written on the gates. There were three gates on each side — east, north, south, and west. The wall of the city had twelve foundation stones, and on them were written the names of the twelve apostles of the Lamb.

The angel who talked to me held in his hand a gold measuring stick to measure the city, its gates, and its wall. When he measured it, he found it was a square, as *wide as it was long. In fact, its length and width and height were each 1,400 miles. Then he measured the walls and found them to be 216 feet thick (according to the human standard used by the angel) The wall was made of jasper, and the city was pure gold, as clear as glass. The wall of the city was built on foundation stones inlaid with twelve precious stones: the first was jasper, the second sapphire, the third agate, the fourth emerald, the fifth onyx, the sixth carnelian, the seventh chrysolite, the eighth beryl, the ninth topaz, the tenth chrysoprase, the eleventh jacinth, the twelfth amethyst.*

The twelve gates were made of pearls — each gate from a single pearl! And the main street was pure gold, as clear as glass.

I saw no temple in the city, for the Lord God Almighty and the Lamb are its temple. And the city has no need of sun or moon, for the glory of God illuminates the city, and the Lamb is its light. The nations will walk in its light, and the kings of the world will enter the city in all their glory. Its gates will never be closed at the end of day because there is no night there. And all the nations will bring their glory and honor into the city. Nothing evil will be allowed to enter, nor anyone who practices shameful idolatry and dishonesty — but only those whose names are written in the Lamb's Book of Life."

7.1 Corporate

Jerusalem is not an organisation. It is not an institution. It is not a Company. It is not a church. We cannot understand Jerusalem if we try to fit her into any of these things. Jerusalem is different from these things as chalk is different to cheese. Where people are seeking to escape from Babylon and explore the Kingdom of God there is a great freedom from the captivity of man's control and organisation.

The vision of John concerning Jerusalem in Revelation is of a future city. There is no sin in this city, nor do the effects of sin cause disharmony. It is probably not possible to find an expression of this city today. We must wait for its future fulfilment before enjoying all it has to offer. But surely, it is worthwhile seeking it now? Individuals inhabit Jerusalem, and they can only gain entrance into the city through Jesus. We have considered the character of those individuals already. A city, though, finds its true character through the interrelationship of its inhabitants. We will consider the impact of these relationships now.

7.2 Unity

Jerusalem is a united city. Unlike the city of Babylon with its many divisions, Jerusalem is a place for people seeking to live in harmony with others. Jesus said in Matthew 5:9 (KJV), *"Blessed are the peace makers for they shall be called the children of God"*.

When writing my previous book, The Unleashed Church, I wrote the following about unity:

> "One day the Holy Spirit gave me a picture of boxes. I was seeing the various church groups as boxes - self-contained with lids. They each had sides, restrictions, and limitations. The lid was the personality figure who was the leader of the church. The sides were the doctrines, personalities, and giftings that drew

people after them. Each had membership control. Each had its own vision and mission. Each held itself to be different from the other boxes. Some were drab, some very colorful, but all were self-reliant.

The Holy Spirit took me again to 1 Corinthians 1 and showed me how the early Church faced similar challenges. Paul's response was clear and applicable to today. There is only one Church. Doctrinal differences are not a valid reason for separation. Personality clashes are not a reason for separation. On the contrary, Jesus, Paul and others spoke of putting divisive people out of the Church. Unity is more important than being right. As we humbly work through our differences, we maintain the purity of relationship and truth.

The boxes stand in opposition to God. It is by our love that the world knows we are disciples of Jesus. The freshness of this old revelation was gripping. Perhaps it carries an urgency as we move deeper into the new season of God. Jesus is the one and only Head of His Church. He holds everything together, not apart. Until we give Him His people and allow Him to hold them together, we live in rebellion to Him.

I saw that the heart of Jesus is to lift off the lid; to pull down the sides of the boxes. He wants to give freedom to His people to explore His wider Body, to enjoy different relationships, and to be able to grow from the wealth and riches He has invested in His people.

I saw that within the boxes people were thin and weak. They were able to grow so far but no further because of the confines of the box. Yet they were hungry for more of Jesus. They were restricted by the lids, unable to enjoy the warmth or life of Jesus found in His Body. Many believed in Body ministry, but could not explore this because the Body was not one to be able to minister together.

I saw that people in different boxes were lonely because their potential God-given relationships were elsewhere. Ministries could not be released, because the working partners were elsewhere. The world was rushing to hell while God's answer, the Church, refused to build an ark for their deliverance.

John Wimber said, "God wants His Church back." He still does. It is not a question of giving the Holy Spirit room in church meetings only, but whether we are prepared to lay down the identity of our church and walk together with humility, love and unity.

I saw that every box stood as a barrier to God and the world. We have no authorization to build a new Church or a different one to the one Jesus is building. He was quite clear to Peter when He said in Matt 16:18 "I will build My church." He said in Luke 12: 32, "It is the Father's good pleasure to give you the kingdom." But the Church is a different matter. He is jealous for His Bride. He died for us; surely, He has the right to fashion us."

My understanding has not changed since writing the above. We can hear the heart of Jesus, just before His crucifixion, as He prayed, "*I pray that they will all be one, just as you and I are one — as you are in me, Father, and I am in you. And may they be in us so that the world will believe you sent me.*"

7.3 Joined together

The people of God are like a net. Again, in my book The Unleashed Church, I wrote:

"A net is full of knots and joints, intertwined and vital. With no joints, the net does not exist. It contains only isolated strands of thread. With joints it is held together and can make a net for holding things. The strength of each joint will determine the potential of the net for holding. Weak joints easily break; holes appear and that which is held will escape or fall away.

Traditionally the Church has been an organization rather than a net, held together by a membership list, doctrine, name, and the personality of the leader. Relationships may exist, but if you leave the box those relationships will be severed, either abruptly because you are no longer following the right way according to the understanding of those few believers. Or over a short time they cease because you are no longer involved in the same vision or activities. The organization brings division, as do doctrines and personality figures.

God's intention is that His people relate with Him and with each other. Without a relationship with God, we have no place in His Body. Without relationship with others in His Body we are not part of the Body. Organization has blinded many people to God's Body. We join an organization and can enjoy the benefits without experiencing relationship. We come to meetings, listen to the music and sermons, and receive from the poor fund. None of these things depends on relationship and none of them is a true reflection of the Body. The Body builds itself up in love as each joint, each muscle, and each sinew plays its part. We are all part of that Body, with no one part being more valuable than another. And as in any body and organism, if we do not exercise the various parts we do not grow in strength.

If God's people had organization taken out of them now, what would be left? The majority would not know what to do to continue with their walk with God. Organization has taken the emphasis away from our relationship with God and each other and placed an unhelpful emphasis on attending meetings, or getting involved in projects and programs instead. Spiritual food is spoon-fed from the front rather than obtained from a living walk with the Holy Spirit.

The Church is relationships. Our baptism into the Body of Christ is the result of relationship with the Father, Son, and Holy Spirit. Our relevance is worked out as our relationship with the Trinity impacts us, changes us and gives us a testimony to share with others. This may be in the form of sharing how we have been changed and helped. It may be manifest as we repeat the revelation we receive as we spend time with God. What He gives to us, we must give away in word or deed. We give away in word, so to touch people's hearts by the power of the Holy Spirit that their lives are changed for good. And we give away by deed, bringing a healing or a miracle, again by the power of the Holy Spirit. All this comes from our relationship with God.

Without relating to others, what we receive from God has nowhere to go. We have to have a superficial relationship at the very least in order to speak to someone or send them a letter. The quality of relationship of God's people is meant to be the best. The world will see Jesus as it sees godly relationships in His people.

The New Testament is full of exhortation and teachings about how to relate and what to do if we break relationship or fellowship (Matt 5:23; Luke 12: 58; Eph 4:25-32 are some examples). The Bible is about covenants between God and man. And He desires that we display a similar covenantal attitude in our relationships, where commitment, honesty, faithfulness, and other godly characteristics overcome the temptation to break relationship. His reason for creating us in the first place was to have relationship. When this was lost through sin, Jesus died to restore that relationship. That is how important relationship is to God. To break relationship brings pain to the whole Body of Christ.

The net of relationships is how the Body of Christ can demonstrate its unity. As we build links - joints - between people living in boxes, the box sides will come down.

History shows that building nets is not successful if it is only at a leadership level. If it is only leaders who build relationship with other leaders the boxes remain as before. If the parts of the Body reach out to others in different boxes transformation will take place. Not only will the strongholds of division be pulled down, but also ministries and giftings will find each other and a serious forward thrust will commence."

Of course, in the future Jerusalem there will be no sin to cause the breakdown of relationships. It is in this age that we need to overcome the temptation to separate from others.

The Apostle Paul in Col 2:19, Eph 2:21, Eph 4:16 and other letters talks about Christians as the Body of Christ. As Christians, we are not individual stones. We are the living stones, placed side by side, to become a temple in which God dwells. We are not individual bones, but joined and supported by the muscles and ligaments.

In a human body, the bones are in a specific formation. Legs are not directly attached to arms. In the same way, each of us in the Body of Christ needs to find our particular place. There should be no malformation in Christ's Church.

Life flows through a natural body when all its parts are in the right place. The heart is beating. The blood is flowing. Yet so often in the spiritual Body of Christ, the life does not flow. The various parts are out of order, often at enmity. We do not know who should be giving us life in the Body. Nor do we know those to whom we should be giving life.

There are many joints - ministry joints, gifting joints, friendship joints, fathers, mothers, brothers, sisters and children joints. We have a place in the family of God where we grow and help others to grow, as well as in the sphere of ministry. Often we will have people around us in the family who are different from the ones we will have in our sphere of ministry. Wherever we are and whatever we do, we need to know who our life-joints are so that the life of God may flow to us and through us effectively.

The more solid and deep our relationships become, the more we will find release into our gifts and ministries. This is not to say we find security in people. Our security can only be centred in God. But we grow in trust of others as we grow in relationship. Many people live their lives without ever finding relationships that go below a superficial level. The Apostle Paul would have thought that strange.

A joint is a place where two bones move together. To a carpenter, a joint is a place where two pieces of wood are locked together. Furniture depends on strong joints to hold what has been made upright and true. Loose joints destroy that. It is the same in the Body of Christ.

7.4 Equality

One of the distinct teachings of the New Testament is that we are equal before God. We can identify this equality in several ways. When writing to the dispersed

Jews, James warns them against discrimination. They were in the habit of giving preferential treatment to rich people over the poor. James reminds them that the people of God are equal before Him and if His people favour some over others, they are committing a sin. He also reminds them that we are equal in being sinners. In James 2 we read, *"My dear brothers and sisters, how can you claim to have faith in our glorious Lord Jesus Christ if you favor some people over others? For example, suppose someone comes into your meeting dressed in fancy clothes and expensive jewellery, and another comes in who is poor and dressed in dirty clothes. If you give special attention and a good seat to the rich person, but you say to the poor one, "You can stand over there, or else sit on the floor" — well, doesn't this discrimination show that your judgments are guided by evil motives? Listen to me, dear brothers and sisters. Hasn't God chosen the poor in this world to be rich in faith? Aren't they the ones who will inherit the Kingdom he promised to those who love him? But you dishonor the poor! Isn't it the rich who oppress you and drag you into court? Aren't they the ones who slander Jesus Christ, whose noble name you bear?*

Yes indeed, it is good when you obey the royal law as found in the Scriptures: "Love your neighbour as yourself." But if you favour some people over others, you are committing a sin. You are guilty of breaking the law. For the person who keeps all of the laws except one is as guilty as a person who has broken all of God's laws. For the same God who said, "You must not commit adultery," also said, "You must not murder." So if you murder someone but do not commit adultery, you have still broken the law. So whatever you say or whatever you do, remember that you will be judged by the law that sets you free. There will be no mercy for those who have not shown mercy to others. But if you have been merciful, God will be merciful when he judges you."

One sin, however small, determines our death unless we have the grace of God. Sin brings us all to the common denominator of being equal failures before God. But

God offers each one the same choice of life instead of death, through faith in the victory of Jesus on the Cross.

In the, so-called, sermon on the mount, Jesus spoke about the need to enter the Kingdom of God through a door. In Matthew 7:13 we read, *"You can enter God's Kingdom only through the narrow gate. The highway to hell is broad, and its gate is wide for the many who choose that way. But the gateway to life is very narrow and the road is difficult, and only a few ever find it."* Later, in Matthew 19:24 we read, *"And again I say unto you, It is easier for a camel to go through the eye of a needle, than for a rich man to enter into the kingdom of God."* Jesus uses the example of a camel entering the city through the gate to emphasise the need for a person to give him or herself fully and unreservedly to Him. An owner of the camel has to take off the baggage from the back of the camel in order for there to be space enough to enter the city. Anyone entering the city has to do so without a bag. It is the same with us when we come to Jesus and ask for entrance to His kingdom. We cannot enter with our own baggage. We come with nothing of value to offer Him other than ourselves. All our wealth, our position, our self-importance, is meaningless. We have to take it off and lay it down in order to receive His forgiveness. It is here that we find equality starts.

Paul encourages equality in the matter of finance. In 1 Corinthians 16, he encourages the habit of putting money aside to give to those in need. Elsewhere, in 2 Corinthians 8:10-14, he explains that he does not want to make those giving to become poor but to bring equality. *"Here is my advice: It would be good for you to finish what you started a year ago. Last year you were the first who wanted to give, and you were the first to begin doing it. Now you should finish what you started. Let the eagerness you showed in the beginning be matched now by your giving. Give in proportion to what you have. Whatever you give is acceptable if you give it eagerly. And give according to what you have, not what you don't have. Of course, I don't mean your giving should make life easy for others and hard for yourselves. I only mean that there should be some equality. Right now you have plenty and can help those who are in need.*

Later, they will have plenty and can share with you when you need it. In this way, things will be equal."

This sense of equality is a common theme throughout the New Testament people of God. In Acts 6, we read the following, *"But as the believers rapidly multiplied, there were rumblings of discontent. The Greek-speaking believers complained about the Hebrew-speaking believers, saying that their widows were being discriminated against in the daily distribution of food. So the Twelve called a meeting of all the believers. They said, "We apostles should spend our time teaching the word of God, not running a food program. And so, brothers, select seven men who are well respected and are full of the Spirit and wisdom. We will give them this responsibility. Then we apostles can spend our time in prayer and teaching the word.""* When the Greek speaking widows complained about their lack of food and about discrimination against them when food was distributed the people of God accepted that was not right and put in motion a plan to bring equality.

This quality of equality should also be seen in the relationships of the people living in spiritual Jerusalem. I wrote the following in the book The Unleashed Church of a picture of a cornfield, which is helpful in illustrating this point.

> "One day I had a picture of a cornfield being blown by the wind. The wind blew and as it touched parts of the field the corn was bent over. As the wind blew so the corn bent. Sometimes whole areas were bending at the same time. Sometimes only a few heads or a limited area would bend, depending on the strength of the wind and the position of the corn.
>
> I was reminded of Jesus' words in John 3:8, "The wind blows wherever it pleases. You hear its sound, but you cannot tell where it comes from or where it is going." God's people are like that. We are a wind-blown people, blown by the breath of the Holy Spirit.
>
> The Holy Spirit seemed to be asking, "Where are the leaders in the cornfield?" This was a difficult

question. I quickly realized that the people of God needed the breath of the Holy Spirit more than they needed leaders. They needed the ability to bend with that breath more than they needed leadership. When the wind of the Holy Spirit blows it is not only the leaders who feel the wind, but everyone born of the Spirit.

The Church should be like the cornfield—a wind-blown people, who are responsive to the Spirit's blowing and not waiting for the leadership to make decisions and give directions. The Church has been manhandled for too long. God wants His Spirit to be the guiding force of all that is done. Acts 9 clearly shows how Ananias, a normal follower of the breath of the Holy Spirit, responded to the Spirit without leadership permission as he went to Saul to lay hands on him for healing of his vision. This was an example of the wind touching a single head of corn, but there are times that this happens with groups also. As the breath of God blew on the day of Pentecost the disciples spilled out onto the street without man's instruction, and so started the great adventure of being blown without knowing the consequences.

God wants His Church to be like a child's kaleidoscope in many respects, always having the same components in terms of gifts, ministries, character, and values. Yet the pattern or picture is constantly changing as the wheel is turned. And it is the hand of God that turns the wheel to change the pattern as and when He wants to. A fluid, flexible, changeable Body of people responds as the wind of the Spirit blows.

Leadership should not be static and hierarchical but dynamic and flowing. Leadership depends on anointing and discerning where the wind of God is blowing. If the Holy Spirit has something to say, that in itself is leadership. Whomever He chooses to blow on to make the words become flesh, are leaders for the duration of time the wind blows on them. This may be untidy to our thinking, but it does give the Lordship and leadership into the province of the Holy Spirit. We are not meant to be in control or know what God is up to all the time. He is a God of surprises. Did the disciples in Acts 2:41 know that 3,000 people would be added to their number as a result of being blown downstairs on the day of Pentecost?

As the wind blows, all God's people should feel His breath bringing life to them - life in abundance. How can we witness to the words of others and confirm them if we do not hear them ourselves (1 Corinthians 14:24)? We commit the same error as did the Israelites. They sought a king in order to be like other nations, and chose Saul to be over them. That is our error when we appoint leaders over us. The gift of leadership (Rom 12:8) is God-given. Like other gifts it is available to all as required, given by the Holy Spirit. People can grow in it and become recognized leaders. But this is not a management role as demonstrated by the world's systems. It is a different style of leader; one who is wind-blown is directed by the Holy Spirit and is a servant to everyone. This leader is one who is not head and shoulders above the rest, but one carrying a towel to wash feet. The leader is not one who is a delegator but a releaser. The leader is not a cork in the bottle to stop things going wrong, but someone who is a part of the Body of Christ with many other leaders walking together. The leader is not one alone but one of many

We are to be a wind-blown people listening to the Spirit of God rather than a man-driven people. The wisdom from above is first peaceable. The wind usually blows in peace. However if He is angry the wind can be fierce. Revelation chapters 2 & 3, show that the whole church suffers if the wind is angry, not just the leaders. Candlesticks are taken away when the people of God resist the breath of God, given by the Holy Spirit."

The cornfield does not require leaders to tell it to bend; it requires the wind. The Holy Spirit dwells in every child of God and is equally available to any who want Him.

There are obvious differences between people: male or female; black or white; those with different gifts. There are many differences, but this should not stop us respecting our equality. In spiritual Jerusalem, there is equality. If we desire to seek God's kingdom, we will seek to bring equality to whomever we become involved.

7.5 Humility

One of the many things that Jesus said about relationships among His people is, *"But among you it will be different. Whoever wants to be a leader among you must be your servant, and whoever wants to be first among you must be the slave of everyone else."* (Mark 10:43-44) He does not say there is no leadership. He says that leadership in His Kingdom is not the same type as in the world. He specifically speaks against hierarchy and the practice of one person being over another. I recently spoke to someone who worked in a large organised Church and was amazed to hear this person say that her husband had – she named the person – as his boss in the Church. I pressed further only to find that she was speaking, as she understood the situation to stand. Someone else in the Church was boss to her husband. This is directly against the teaching of Jesus.

There is a place for leadership. It is not above, nor is it below, for that would also create hierarchy. It is alongside. Leaders in the Kingdom of God are not like those in the world's organisations who use position to obtain their own way. Instead, they are examples of how to live. They are available to give advice and to show how to care for each other. They are growing in spiritual maturity and recognised by others as replicas of Jesus.

Elders are people that others consider are worthy of respect. They have proved their honesty, and credibility, by their life style and reflection of Jesus. They lead by example and are available to help others to be like Jesus. They do not have the right or the expectation, if they have the heart of Jesus, to be obeyed automatically. Nonetheless, people will respect their opinions and, because those opinions demonstrate the heart of God, they will be happy to follow the advice given. There are some verses in the bible that seem to suggest that leaders have authority by being above others, but a closer investigation of the meaning and roots of these verses shows they have been misunderstood historically. Many others, with an understanding of the Greek and Hebrew texts, have demonstrated this elsewhere but I have added an appendix 3 to give some simple understanding.

Leaders also carry a responsibility to be "overseers". This is the ability to see what is happening in the spirit beyond the ability of less mature Christians. By seeing in this way they are able to see danger coming and give warning; they can care for the people of God by being hearers in the spirit.

Having made these introductory statements about leadership, we see that any inhabitant of Jerusalem will be humble. Jesus came to earth and took on the form of a servant. (Philippians 2) He did not come to bully or coerce but to serve the people He met. He was the model of humility. A dictionary definition of humility is *"the quality or condition of being humble; modest opinion or estimate of one's own importance, rank, etc."* Humility accepts that "I" am not as important as the Spirit of God, regardless with whom He chooses to reside.

7.6 Gifted

In the vision that John saw, as described in the book of Revelation, there will be no requirement for gifts. The purpose of gifts of the Spirit is to equip the people of God now in preparation for the final age. But it is helpful to consider how God is preparing His people for that day. In 1 Cor 12, Paul discusses the variety of gifts and services within the people of God. We read, *"Now, dear brothers and sisters, regarding your question about the special abilities the Spirit gives us. I don't want you to misunderstand this. You know that when you were still pagans, you were led astray and swept along in worshipping speechless idols. So I want you to know that no one speaking by the Spirit of God will curse Jesus, and no one can say Jesus is Lord, except by the Holy Spirit. There are different kinds of spiritual gifts, but the same Spirit is the source of them all. There are different kinds of service, but we serve the same Lord. God works in different ways, but it is the same God who does the work in all of us.*

A spiritual gift is given to each of us so we can help each other. To one person the Spirit gives the ability to give wise advice; to another the same Spirit gives a message of special knowledge. The same Spirit gives great faith to another, and to someone else the one Spirit gives the gift of healing. He gives one person the power to perform miracles, and another the ability to prophesy. He gives someone else the ability to discern whether a message is from the Spirit of God or from another spirit. Still another person is given the ability to speak in unknown languages, while another is given the ability to interpret what is being said. It is the one and only Spirit who distributes all these gifts. He alone decides which gift each person should have."

Paul stresses that it is the responsibility of the Holy Spirit to give gifts to people. Equally, he stresses that everyone may receive these gifts. Whether the gifts are permanent or temporary is not clear from this particular passage but it is clear that everyone who has received the Spirit of God also receives gifts.

Jesus made the same point when He told the parable of the talents. In Mathew 25:14-30 we read, "*Again, the Kingdom of Heaven can be illustrated by the story of a man going on a long trip. He called together his servants and entrusted his money to them while he was gone. He gave five bags of silver to one, two bags of silver to another and one bag of silver to the last — dividing it in proportion to their abilities. He then left on his trip. The servant who received the five bags of silver began to invest the money and earned five more. The servant with two bags of silver also went to work and earned two more. But the servant who received the one bag of silver dug a hole in the ground and hid the master's money.*

"After a long time their master returned from his trip and called them to give an account of how they had used his money. The servant to whom he had entrusted the five bags of silver came forward with five more and said, 'Master, you gave me five bags of silver to invest, and I have earned five more.'

"The master was full of praise. 'Well done, my good and faithful servant. You have been faithful in handling this small amount, so now I will give you many more responsibilities. Let's celebrate together!' "The servant who had received the two bags of silver came forward and said, 'Master, you gave me two bags of silver to invest, and I have earned two more.' "The master said, 'Well done, my good and faithful servant. You have been faithful in handling this small amount, so now I will give you many more responsibilities. Let's celebrate together!'

"Then the servant with the one bag of silver came and said, 'Master, I knew you were a harsh man, harvesting crops you didn't plant and gathering crops you didn't cultivate. I was afraid I would lose your money, so I hid it in the earth. Look, here is your money back.' "But the master replied, 'You wicked and lazy servant! If you knew I harvested crops I didn't plant and gathered crops I didn't cultivate, why didn't you deposit my money in the bank? At least I could have gotten some interest on it.' "Then he ordered, 'Take the money from this servant, *and give it to the one with the ten bags of silver. To those who use well what they are given, even more will be given, and they will have an abundance. But from those who do nothing, even what little they have will be taken away. Now throw this useless servant into outer darkness, where there will be weeping and gnashing of teeth.'"*

In this parable, Jesus taught that each servant receives at least one gift. Although each servant received a different amount, each had something. There was equality in status, but variety in gifts. Each servant had the same responsibility however - to use the gifts wisely. We can learn much from what Jesus taught in that parable. It was the servant who had fewest gifts, but failed to use them wisely, who was punished. Today, in many Church groups, many people consider they have no gifts and leave the "work of ministry" to a select few "multi-gifted" people. Jesus taught that this attitude would result in great loss to the individuals concerned.

The Holy Spirit gives every child of God gifts. Sometimes a gift may be temporary, given for a specific purpose at a specific time, such as a prophetic word or word of knowledge. Or a gift may be a more permanent, one that develops with use so that the person involved becomes recognised as one who is skilful in its use.

The purpose of gifts is to build up and encourage others. If some one is wealthy, he or she should use the wealth to assist others as the Spirit leads them. If the gift is prophecy, he or she should seek ways to encourage and build up. The gifts are not tools to destroy others. They are to assist the people of God to become united, mature, and a blessing. We saw in the teaching of Jesus that He expects the users of gifts to invest wisely. This speaks of reproduction and growth. No gift is of any value unless it produces fruit. Jesus taught that a person who does not use the gift would suffer loss.

The people of God are gifted. Jerusalem is full of gifted people. All we have is a gift from God. Eternal life is a gift. And the gifts of the Spirit come from the eternal life that we have been given.

7.7 Meetings

There are times when people meet together. This is encouraged by the New Testament writers but there is much confusion about what this means. Many go to services, when a group follows a programme with prepared readings, prayers, and songs. But, God's people do not need services and God does not want services. They are a form of temple worship similar to that offered to the heathen gods of Rome and Greece. They achieved nothing then and achieve little if anything now.

Many follow a pattern of rousing singing followed by a lecture – a "sermon" or exegesis. All too often, though, they achieve little – which is not to say that the Holy Spirit is incapable of touching the hearts of men and women when they hear an explanation of God's Word. But, often that is so rare as to be the exception rather than the rule. There is much similarity in the "worhip groups" to secular bands, and the mass hysteria they induce in these gatherings has little spiritual value and there is no New Testament basis for meeting in this way.

In fact, there is limited New Testament reference to meetings. Paul spoke to the Ephesians at length just before he left for the last time. He spoke all night because he had much to say. We can deduce from this that there may be some basis for having times of teaching. It is not every week, but when the Holy Spirit has something to say. Normally this becomes obvious because several people start talking about the same thing. When the Holy Spirit wants to talk, He talks to several people. This enables Him to confirm that He is talking; that it is not just the imagination of a mere person.

There are many accounts of open-air discussions in the New Testament. Clearly, the place to preach the gospel was often the open air, not inside a hall, but the open air in Ephesus and the Middle East generally is warm and more helpful for this than an English winter. Paul also says that people will be convicted as they listen to prophecy in a house, so that is another place to share good news – and a comfort to us in a colder climate.

In 1 Corinthians 14:26-33, Paul gives the clearest account of what happens when we meet together. Nowhere does he say how frequently this is, or how well the people knew each other. In my experience, this type of meeting can be between people who know each other well or between those who have just met. It does not depend on personal relationship but on spiritual relationship.

It does not have to be a regular meeting between the same people. In fact, much of what God is doing today does not seem to involve regular meetings together. People are building relationships across the spectrum of the people of God. Meetings are taking place between two people or fifteen. Jesus said that the smallest group that can have a meeting can be two people – so long as He is there as well. It is not size that attracts God, but people who are seeking Him.

In 1 Corinthians 14:26-33, Paul says, "*When you meet together, one will sing, another will teach, another will tell some special revelation God has given, one will speak in tongues, and another will interpret what is said. But everything that is done must strengthen all of you.*

No more than two or three should speak in tongues. They must speak one at a time, and someone must interpret what they say. But if no one is present who can interpret, they must be silent in your church meeting and speak in tongues to God privately.

Let two or three people prophesy, and let the others evaluate what is said. But if someone is prophesying and another person receives a revelation from the Lord, the one who is speaking must stop. In this way, all who prophesy will have a turn to speak, one after the other, so that everyone will learn and be encouraged. Remember that people who prophesy are in control of their spirit and can take turns. For God is not a God of disorder but of peace, as in all the meetings of God's holy people."

Paul says that everyone is speaking in his or her turn. One person will sing, not everyone. This is probably a prophetic song or one of encouragement. It is not community hymn singing. Someone may teach, someone else share a revelation, a tongue, a prophecy etc. Everything is coming from the Holy Spirit. God is speaking to, and through, His people.

When I visit houses, there are often several people present. If I have something I believe the Holy Spirit wants me to share, I will often ask people what God is saying to them. This achieves two things. It confirms that I am on track (assuming people confirm my message). It also releases faith to receive what the Holy Spirit is saying. If God is talking, we are foolish to ignore Him.

When in Kenya in 2011, I was visiting a school. Afterwards, the school headmistress took us to her home where we met around thirty people; many being a new face to me. The group, many being new to each other as well as me, asked me to share. I started by asking if anyone had anything they wished to share, perhaps a dream or prophecy, or whatever was stirring them. Several people spoke confirming the word I had. One had a dream that described the word exactly, although they knew nothing of it at all.

What I am trying to stress is that we can meet anywhere. There is nothing sacred about a house or a building. A house is convenient but so is a coffee shop if we meet in town. Paul encourages us to lift up hands anywhere in prayer (1 Tim). I am not sure that lifting up hands is helpful today, but praying certainly is.

The purpose of meeting is to build each other up. This can be over a meal or not. The fewer the better usually. A large crowd will squash out many people and only the confident will speak. We can meet to talk, to study the bible, to pray, make decisions. So long as they are God - speaking times, and we are seeking to serve each other meet as often as possible. They are not usually formal times though, but times of informal relationship around the Holy Spirit.

7.8 The presence of God

No discussion of Jerusalem can be complete without an emphasis on God. He is the architect of this city. He has the patience and love to bring it to pass. The city that God offers is unlike any that man can build. God fills the city. Love is the atmosphere. Light is His glory. There is no sin found there, nor the consequences of sin. There is no fear, no sickness, no sorrow. The presence of God fills everything, and everywhere.

We cannot imagine what it will be like to live in an environment without the pollution of sin; where there is no fear. But, this is the place that is in the heart of God and that He offers to any who respond to Him.

Appendix1

Is tithing a requirement for Christians?

Did Jesus tithe? The Bible does not tell us the answer to this question but does give insight into His practice and thinking about similar issues. In Matthew 17:24-27 we read the following *"On their arrival in Capernaum, the collectors of the Temple tax came to Peter and asked him, "Doesn't your teacher pay the Temple tax?" "Yes, he does," Peter replied. Then he went into the house. But before he had a chance to speak, Jesus asked him, "What do you think, Peter? Do kings tax their own people or the people they have conquered?" "They tax the people they have conquered," Peter replied. "Well, then," Jesus said, "the citizens are free! However, we don't want to offend them, so go down to the lake and throw in a line. Open the mouth of the first fish you catch, and you will find a large silver coin. Take it and pay the tax for both of us."*

Jesus did not expect to pay the Temple tax because He is the king of the kingdom to which the temple was subject. He also includes His followers in that expectation that the tax does not apply to them. This passage raises an interesting insight into the attitude of Jesus. He does not consider Himself or His followers subject to the rules of the religious rulers. A religious requirement has no hold over Him or them.

Tithing is first mentioned in Genesis 14:19-21 after Abraham had won a significant battle over several regional kings. The passage reads as follows, *"Melchizedek blessed Abram with this blessing: "Blessed be Abram by God Most High, Creator of heaven and earth. And blessed be God Most High, who has defeated your enemies for you." Then Abram gave Melchizedek a tenth of all the goods he had recovered.*

Melchizedek is called a High Priest and Jesus is given the title "High Priest after the order of Melchizedek" by the writer of Hebrews (Heb 5:9-10) as follows: *"In this way, God qualified him as a perfect High Priest, and he became the source of eternal salvation for all those who obey him. And God designated him to be a High Priest in the order of Melchizedek.*"

Abraham gave a tenth, or a tithe, of his battle trophies to Melchizedek - a person symbolising God himself. Jesus was of the same order as Melchizedek, showing his divine nature. It seems that Abraham recognised this characteristic and gave his tithe to God. It was a one-off event and we do not read he ever tithed in this way before or afterwards. On this occasion, Abraham gave a tenth of the spoils of war; of stolen goods. In summary, Abraham tithed once in his life, directly to God and out of stolen goods. Although the first time tithing is mentioned, this is not really a good passage from which to develop a doctrine of tithing.

Two generations later, as Jacob is running away from Isaac he comes to Bethel and makes a covenant with God as follows in Genesis 28:21-22: "*and if I return safely to my father's home, then the Lord will certainly be my God. And this memorial pillar I have set up will become a place for worshipping God, and I will present to God a tenth of everything he gives me.*" Jacob also tithed on one occasion directly to God. The tithing idea seemed to miss Isaac totally.

The number ten has much significance to the Nation of Israel. God uses the number on many occasions in His requirements for the people. It speaks of a particular characteristic in man's relationship to Him. It was on the tenth day that God delivered the nation from Egypt (Exodus 12:3). It was used as a measurement when collecting manna - the container used to measure the manna was an omer, one tenth of an ephah, holding about two quarts (Exodus 16:36). It was on the tenth day that the Day of Atonement was to be celebrated (Leviticus 23:27). As in much of the Old Testament, God was using a picture to point to and prepare the way for Jesus. The tenth is a picture of Jesus' humanity and His victory through dependence on His Father. The tenth defines our dependence on God as people who have not yet experienced His work of salvation. God used the number ten to show man that he was dependent on Him especially for decisions of Government.

In the books of Leviticus, Numbers, and Deuteronomy, there are several passages concerning tithing. They describe God's involvement with His people. He lives with them and has ownership within their lands. But He has not yet been given the position as the King - even though He is Almighty God. Jesus accomplished the finished work. In Leviticus 27:30-32 we read, *"One tenth of the produce of the land, whether grain from the fields or fruit from the trees, belongs to the Lord and must be set apart to him as holy. If you want to buy back the Lord's tenth of the grain or fruit, you must pay its value, plus 20 percent. Count off every tenth animal from your herds and flocks and set them apart for the Lord as holy."* In verse 31, we find that people could buy back the tithe to the Lord of grain or fruit after they had first given it to Him.

The priests received some of the tithe. The reason for this was that they were not allowed to own land; the tithe enabled them to live. They were required to give a tenth of that tithe to the Lord. This is confirmed in Numbers 18:26, *"Give these instructions to the Levites: When you receive from the people of Israel the tithes I have assigned as your allotment, give a tenth of the tithes you receive - a tithe of the tithe - to the Lord as a sacred offering."* Today, of course, there is no separate priest caste to which to tithe. We are all priests.

The tithe was a requirement for the nation of Israel as laid down by God during their travels in the wilderness. The nation followed this practice until the time of Jesus although not very diligently. The book of Malachi tells of God's displeasure that the nation had stopped giving Him the tithe during his lifetime. However, Jesus mentions the practice when talking to the strict teachers and Pharisees as we read in Matthew 23:23. *"What sorrow awaits you teachers of religious law and you Pharisees? Hypocrites! For you are careful to tithe even the tiniest income from your herb gardens, but you ignore the more important aspects of the law - justice, mercy, and faith. You should tithe, yes, but do not neglect the more important things"*. He agrees they should tithe but says there were important things they were neglecting. They should tithe because they were of the nation of Israel.

Jesus did not expect to tithe nor pay the temple tax as we noticed earlier. He told Peter that the sons are free, and not bound by the requirement for taxation to the Temple. We are those sons.

Jesus makes a clear statement in Matthew 5:17-18, *"Don't misunderstand why I have come. I did not come to abolish the Law of Moses or the writings of the prophets. No, I came to accomplish their purpose. I tell you the truth, until heaven and earth disappear, not even the smallest detail of God's law will disappear until its purpose is achieved."* Jesus came to fulfill the purpose of the law and He did this through His life, death, and resurrection. He fulfilled the purpose of the tithe and it no longer has any purpose, unless it is to point those who do not know Him towards Jesus.

The NT says nothing more about the tithe until we reach the book of Hebrews, a book written to Jews who followed Jesus. Nowhere does the writer say that tithing is still required, but he does write about the tenth given by Abraham to Melchizedek; not for the development of understanding tithing but in order to understand the character of Jesus more (Hebrews 7).

There are several occasions when the NT would have mentioned tithing if followers of Jesus had still practiced it. In Acts 5, we read of an incident concerning the sale of a field by Ananias and his wife Sapphira. *"But there was a certain man named Ananias who, with his wife, Sapphira, sold some property. He brought part of the money to the apostles, claiming it was the full amount. With his wife's consent, he kept the rest. Then Peter said, "Ananias, why have you let Satan fill your heart? You lied to the Holy Spirit, and you kept some of the money for yourself. The property was yours to sell or not sell, as you wished. And after selling it, the money was also yours to give away. How could you do a thing like this? You weren't lying to us but to God!" As soon as Ananias heard these words, he fell to the floor and died. Everyone who heard about it was terrified. Then some young men got up, wrapped him in a sheet, and took him out and buried him. About three hours later his wife came in, not knowing what had happened. Peter asked her, "Was this the price you and your husband received for your land?" "Yes," she replied, "that was the price." And Peter said, "How could the two of you even think of conspiring to test the Spirit of the Lord like this? The young men who buried your husband are just outside the door, and they will carry you out, too." Instantly, she fell to the floor and died. When the young men came in and saw that she was dead, they carried her out and buried her beside her husband. Great fear gripped the entire church and everyone else who heard what had happened."*

This incident occurred when the followers of Jesus were giving away their wealth to each other. A fellow believer, Barnabas, had sold land and given away 100% of the proceeds. Ananias and his wife wanted to look good and decided to pretend to do the same. If tithing were still a practice, it would be inconceivable that there would be a problem. They would have tithed and kept the rest but it seems this was not the case. They were unwilling to give away 100% and determined to lie about the decision. As Peter said, the money was theirs and there was no requirement to give any away.

Paul would have mentioned tithing when writing to the followers of Jesus asking for a collection to be made so that the people suffering in the famine could be assisted. He makes no mention of the practice at all but encourages people to give generously. 1 Corinthians 16:1-4 says, *"Now regarding your question about the money being collected for God's people in Jerusalem. You should follow the same procedure I gave to the churches in Galatia. On the first day of each week, you should each put aside a portion of the money you have earned. Don't wait until I get there and then try to collect it all at once. When I come, I will write letters of recommendation for the messengers you choose to deliver your gift to Jerusalem. And if it seems appropriate for me to go along, they can travel with me."*

In summary, the requirement to tithe does not apply to followers of Jesus. It was a requirement for the nation of Israel before the time of Jesus – a requirement Jesus fulfilled through His life, death, and resurrection. There never was a requirement for Gentiles to tithe.

Appendix 2

Does the New Testament recommend paid workers?

In 1 Cor 9: 3-23 Paul states, "*This is my answer to those who question my authority. Don't we have the right to live in your homes and share your meals? Don't we have the right to bring a Christian wife with us as the other apostles and the Lord's brothers do, and as Peter does? Or is it only Barnabas and I who have to work to support ourselves?*

What soldier has to pay his own expenses? What farmer plants a vineyard and doesn't have the right to eat some of its fruit? What shepherd cares for a flock of sheep and isn't allowed to drink some of the milk? Am I expressing merely a human opinion, or does the law say the same thing? For the Law of Moses says, "You must not muzzle an ox to keep it from eating as it treads out the grain." Was God thinking only about oxen when he said this? Wasn't he actually speaking to us? Yes, it was written for us, so that the one who ploughs and the one who threshes the grain might both expect a share of the harvest.

Since we have planted spiritual seed among you, aren't we entitled to a harvest of physical food and drink? If you support others who preach to you, shouldn't we have an even greater right to be supported? But we have never used this right. We would rather put up with anything than be an obstacle to the Good News about Christ.

Don't you realize that those who work in the temple get their meals from the offerings brought to the temple? And those who serve at the altar get a share of the sacrificial offerings. In the same way, the Lord ordered that those who preach the Good News should be supported by those who benefit from it. Yet I have never used any of these rights. And I am not writing this to suggest that I want to start now. In fact, I would rather die than lose my right to boast about preaching without charge. Yet preaching the Good News is not something I can boast about. I am compelled by God to do it. How terrible for me if I didn't preach the Good News!

If I were doing this on my own initiative, I would deserve payment. But I have no choice, for God has given me this sacred trust. What then is my pay? It is the opportunity to preach the Good News without charging anyone. That's why I never demand my rights when I preach the Good News.

Even though I am a free man with no master, I have become a slave to all people to bring many to Christ. When I was with the Jews, I lived like a Jew to bring the Jews to Christ. When I was with those who follow the Jewish law, I too lived under that law. Even though I am not subject to the law, I did this so I could bring to Christ those who are under the law. When I am with the Gentiles who do not follow the Jewish law, I too live apart from that law so I can bring them to Christ. But I do not ignore the law of God; I obey the law of Christ.

When I am with those who are weak, I share their weakness, for I want to bring the weak to Christ. Yes, I

*try to find common ground with everyone, doing
everything I can to save some. I do everything to spread
the Good News and share in its blessings."*

Paul did not take money to cover his expenses when
travelling from country to country. On the contrary, he
worked as a tent maker to pay for himself, his fellow
travellers, and the people he visited. He sought to be a
blessing, not a drain on their resources. He seems to have
been criticised for this approach and makes his defence
in the passage above.

The examples he uses are of temporary payment for
work not permanent. His master, or the people he fights
for, pays the soldier. Having fought he moves on to the
next master. A farmer and shepherd eats and drinks in
the season of harvest. An ox eats the grain that it is
threshing only for a short time.

We are all priests and are able to share in the offerings.
There should no longer be a separate priest group, who
take for themselves privileges over others. There are
people who take on a task for a season such as going to a

distant place to evangelise and are unable to earn a living whilst there. Local supporters could assist them for a short time whilst they are there. If the visit becomes permanent, however they should obtain work, so that they do not burden local people. Paul was talking about such people in the passage above.

A permanent paid worker does not have, and never has had, a place in a local group. The only reason for paying someone is when he or she is in a place on a short-term basis without the opportunity to work. It is not payment for a position but for a service rendered; out of love, not requirement.

Many people refer to the fact that Jesus held a common bag to show validation for paid workers. I do not think this is wise. He was a traveller and had many travelling with Him. The wealthy women and others who wanted to assist supported Him. The disciples used the common bag to feed others as well as themselves. When Jesus responded to the need to feed the five thousand, He suggested to His disciples that they might do the job, perhaps thinking about the common purse. In any event, the common purse did not always meet their needs; for example, there was nothing in it to pay the Temple tax when required.

Appendix 3

Leadership

Jesus taught that anyone who followed Him should not call anyone else Lord, Father, or Master. This seems very simple and easy to grasp, but the majority of Christians follow a different teaching. We find the teaching of Jesus on this matter in Matthew 23:9, *"And don't address anyone here on earth as 'Father,' for only God in heaven is your spiritual Father."*

Also, in Mark 10:42-45. *"So Jesus called them together and said, "You know that the rulers in this world lord it over their people, and officials flaunt their authority over those under them. But among you it will be different. Whoever wants to be a leader among you must be your servant, and whoever wants to be first among you must be the slave of everyone else. For even the Son of Man came not to be served but to serve others and to give his life as a ransom for many."*

There seems to be a paradox here to our western minds. We must not look to others for seniority, but it is possible to be a leader. In fact, Jesus is stressing the need to have a right attitude to others. A common problem with leaders is that they become elevated above the people they seek to lead, whether through their choice or that of others. He addressed this problem in two ways. First, He spoke to the people in the Matthew 23 quote above and told them that they must not elevate anyone to a position above them. Second, in Mark 10, He spoke to anyone wishing to be a leader and spoke about his or her heart. It must be a servant heart.

Leadership in the New Testament, as applied to the people of God, always relates to time, not hierarchy. People who lead are those who do things first or who arrive first in a location.

Consider for a moment the teaching of the followers of Jesus - people like Paul, Peter, and John. Their approach to leadership is that of Jesus but there are some confusing passages that seem to indicate otherwise, although much of the confusion arises from poor translations of what the writers originally said.

For example, in 1 Corinthians 12:27-31, Paul says, *"All of you together are Christ's body, and each of you is a part of it. Here are some of the parts God has appointed for the church: first are apostles, second are prophets, third are teachers, then those who do miracles, those who have the gift of healing, those who can help others, those who have the gift of leadership, those who speak in unknown languages. Are we all apostles? Are we all prophets? Are we all teachers? Do we all have the power to do miracles? Do we all have the gift of healing? Do we all have the ability to speak in unknown languages? Do we all have the ability to interpret unknown languages? Of course not! So you should earnestly desire the most helpful gifts. But now let me show you a way of life that is best of all."*

Following a section in which he is stressing the importance of harmony and recognising everyone in the body of Christ, what Paul is doing is highlighting some gifts that demonstrate his point. There are many parts in the body. There are many gifts. Everyone is different. The apostolic gift is first in time in a situation. God sends this gift to break open a place and lay a foundation of Jesus Christ. The prophetic gift follows, to help lay this foundation and to speak clear words of direction and understanding to the people of God. Then comes the teaching gift to reinforce what has been laid, and to bring understanding. After that come many gifts in no particular order.

It is only because of the institutionalisation of the church that these verses have been understood as hierarchical. It is only because of the institutionalisation of the church that there is any need for hierarchy.

Earlier, in 1 Corinthians 11:2-16, Paul says "*I am so glad that you always keep me in your thoughts, and that you are following the teachings I passed on to you. But there is one thing I want you to know: The head of every man is Christ, the head of woman is man, and the head of Christ is God. A man dishonours his head if he covers his head while praying or prophesying. But a woman dishonours her head if she prays or prophesies without a covering on her head, for this is the same as shaving her head. Yes, if she refuses to wear a head covering, she should cut off all her hair! But since it is shameful for a woman to have her hair cut or her head shaved, she should wear a covering. A man should not wear anything on his head when worshiping, for man is made in God's image and reflects God's glory. And woman reflects man's glory. For the first man didn't come from woman, but the first woman came from man. And man was not made for woman, but woman was made for man. For this reason, and because the angels are watching, a woman should wear a covering on her head to show she is under authority. But among the Lord's people, women are not independent of men, and men are not independent of women. For although the first woman came from man, every other man was born from a woman, and everything comes from God.*

Judge for yourselves. Is it right for a woman to pray to God in public without covering her head? Isn't it obvious that it's disgraceful for a man to have long hair? And isn't long hair a woman's pride and joy? For it has been given to her as a covering. But if anyone wants to argue about this, I simply say that we have no other custom than this, and neither do God's other churches."

That passage has been used to undermine women for centuries because it is read as if Paul is stating his belief. But, when the verses are read differently, however, their meaning becomes clear.

Paul had a method of writing that was common in his day and is repeated in certain circumstances in our day. His habit was to repeat a question he had been asked before giving his response. When at school, I followed the same routine. In an exam, I wrote the question asked at the top of the page and then answered to the best of my ability. The difficulty with Paul is that we do not have the letters he received and do not know the questions asked. To some extent this is irrelevant as Paul helpfully wrote the question in his letters, but it would help us immensely if we could see that in other documents.

The Corinthians asked Paul about heads, head coverings, and other things. Paul writes the question. It is clearly not his belief. His practice in other situations does not follow what he writes, and his statements are not true. Among other things, a man did not dishonour his head whilst praying with his head covered. The Jewish practice is to have a cap on whilst praying.

Having written the question, Paul says *"But among the Lord's people, women are not independent of men, and men are not independent of women. For although the first woman came from man, every other man was born from a woman, and everything comes from God."* He starts by saying "but". He compares what the Corinthians believe with what he believes. God's people are not independent, not hierarchical, but interdependent. Man may have come first but every man born since has depended on a woman for the birth to take place. He is putting men in their place – alongside women, not above them.

Paul then writes another question, which deals with the length of hair. Again, there are statements that cannot be Paul's belief. He was a Jew. Long hair was expected: rather than a disgrace, it was a sign of religious zeal. For example, Nazarites were not allowed to cut their hair. Samson lost his strength because he did cut his hair. The High Priest was not allowed to cut his hair and Paul himself made a vow that he would not cut his hair for a long time. This is clearly not a statement of his belief.

Paul's belief was that men and women are interdependent. There is no hierarchy with man on top of the pile.

Peter had the same understanding. He lived with Jesus and understood the principles of the Kingdom of God. In his epistle, 1 Peter 5:5, he says "*And now, a word to you who are elders in the churches. I, too, am an elder and a witness to the sufferings of Christ. And I, too, will share in his glory when he is revealed to the whole world. As a fellow elder, I appeal to you: Care for the flock that God has entrusted to you. Watch over it willingly, not grudgingly — not for what you will get out of it, but because you are eager to serve God. Don't lord it over the people assigned to your care, but lead them by your own good example. And when the Great Shepherd appears, you will receive a crown of never-ending glory and honour. In the same way, you younger men must accept the authority of the elders. And all of you, serve each other in humility, for "God opposes the proud but favours the humble."*

In this passage, the translators have tended to stress the authority of the elders rather than the need to be teachable. The context is the need to serve each other because God opposes the proud. It seems a little strange that Peter would insist on formal submission to a leader when he is stressing serving each other. What Peter is saying here is that younger men should be willing to yield to the wisdom of the more mature ones. He does not seek to set up hierarchy but to encourage a willingness to listen to each other, to serve each other, and to maintain harmony.